RISING EAST: *The Journal of East London Studies*

Volume One *Number One*

Chair
    Michael Rustin
    Dean of the Faculty
    of Social Sciences, UEL

Editor
    Tim Butler
    Department of Sociology, UEL

Assistant Editor
    Ruth Borthwick

Editor, Trends East
    Vikki Rix

Editorial Board
    David Albury
    Office for Public Management

    Phil Cohen
    Centre for New Ethnicities
    Research, UEL

    Sunny Crouch
    London Docklands
    Development Corporation

    Steve Crow
    London East TEC

    David Edgar
    Head of Finance, UEL

    Victor Farlie
    London East TEC

    Bill Hahn
    The London Lee Valley
    Partnership

    Robert Home
    Department of Surveying, UEL

    Steve Jacobs
    Stratford Development Partnership

    Margaret O'Brien
    University of North London

    Alice Sampson
    Centre for Institutional Studies, UEL

    Carole Snee
    Head of Regeneration Office, UEL

    Drew Stevenson
    Faculty of Social Sciences, UEL

    Steven Timms
    Member of Parliament

    Anna Whyatt
    Faculty of Social Sciences, UEL

Rising East: The Journal of East London Studies is published three times a year by Lawrence & Wishart on behalf of the University of East London. The university acknowledges the generous contribution of the London East Training and Enterprise (LETEC) in co-funding this journal.

Text design by Jan Brown
Text setting Art Services, Norwich
Marketing consultant, Jonathan Keane

Subscriptions

For 1997, subscription rates are:
UK: Individuals £20,
Institutions £50,
Corporate Subscribers £100,
Rest of the world: Individuals £30,
Institutions £60,
Corporate Subscribers £110.
Single copies £10

All subscriptions administered by:

Lawrence & Wishart
99a Wallis Road, London E9 5LN
Tel: 0181 533 2506
Fax: 0181 533 7369

Contributions, correpondence and books for review

Send to: Tim Butler, Editor, *Rising East: The Journal of East London Studies*, Department of Sociology, University of East London, Longbridge Road, Dagenham RM8 2AS.

Prospective writers are encouraged to contact the editors to discuss their ideas and to obtain a copy of our style sheet.

Collection as a whole © Rising East 1997
Individual articles the © authors 1997

No article may be reproduced or transmitted by any means, electronic or mechanical, including photocopying, recording or any information storage and retrieval system, without the permission in writing of the publisher, editor or author

ISSN 1367 787X
ISBN 0 85315 846 0

Printed in Great Britain by Cambridge University Press, Cambridge

Contents

Volume 1: Issue 1

iv   Notes on Contributors

vii	*Tim Butler*	Editorial: Giving voice to the sub-region
15	*Drew Stevenson*	Structuring Change in the Sub-region: values, vision and governance in East London
36	*Anna Whyatt*	Thames Gateway London in the Millennium
59	*Robert Home*	Building a Mosque in Stepney: ethnic minorities and the planning system
78	*Caroline Knowles*	Race and Place in 'Schizophrenic' Narratives
97	*Margaret O'Brien & Deborah Jones*	Young People, Family Life and Education in Barking and Dagenham: three case studies

TRENDS EAST

118	Vikki Rix	Industrial Decline, Economic Restructuring and Social Exclusion in London East, 1980s and 1990s

ARTY FACTS

142	Ken Worpole	The Talking Cure: Harold Pinter and the voices of East End writers
148	Bruce Jerram & Richard Wells	Having a Wonderful Time: on developing a visitor economy for East London
164	Roger Mills	The Art of Cable Street

REVIEWS

175   Carole Satyamurti *A Good Death*

Notes on Contributors

Tim Butler is Principal Lecturer in Sociology at the University of East London. He co-edited, with Michael Rustin, *Rising in the East? The regeneration of East London* (1996) and is writing a book on gentrification and the middle classes.

Drew Stevenson's background is in town planning and local government. He was Head of Policy Planning at the GLC and has nearly thirty years' experience of London local government. He is Chair of Urban Regeneration at University of East London.

Anna Whyatt is Principal Research Fellow, University of East London. She was Chief Executive of Southwark (1985-1994) and is a council member of London First and the Industrial Society. She was project director for the London TEC's *An Economic Profile of London*.

Robert Home is Reader in Planning at the School of Surveying, University of East London. He was formerly a member of the Royal Town Planning Institute's Equal Opportunities (Race) Panel and has published a book on colonial town planning. He is currently writing on the planning history of East London.

Caroline Knowles is Professor in the Department of Sociology and Anthropology at Concordia University in Montreal. She is author of *Family Boundaries: the Invention of Normality and Dangerousness*, 1996.

Margaret O'Brien is Professor in Family Studies and Head of School of Social Work at the University of North London. She has co-edited, with Julia Brannen, *Children and Families: Research and Policy* and is now working on a new project on childhood and urban regeneration.

Deborah Jones is Research Fellow at the University of North London. She has worked on the project 'Family and Kinship in Barking and Dagenham' for three years. Her research interests lie in the field of family studies and intergenerational patterns of behaviour.

Vikki Rix is Research Fellow in the Department of Sociology at the University of East London. She has worked extensively on analysing social and economic change within the London East sub-region and is joint author, with Michael Rustin and Prue Chamberlayne, of a forthcoming book on contemporary European societies.

Ken Worpole is a writer who has lived in Hackney for nearly thirty years. His most recent book, *Staying Close to the River* (1995) is an urban travel diary, recording visits to many different cities and quarters of the world, including Moscow, Barcelona, Darwin, Donegal and Dalston.

Bruce Jerram works in the faculty of Social Sciences at UEL. He recently contributed to a study of the tourism potential of the Thames Gateway, for LETEC, and co-authored an article on tourism and the North London Line in *Rising in the East* (1996).

Richard Wells now works at the UEL Faculty of Social Sciences, having previously been employed as a museum director. He is co-author of an article on tourism and East London in *Rising in the East* (1996).

Roger Mills is the author of several novels for teenagers, including *Bad Fun* and *The Tarnished Wings of Angels*. He is the Literature Development Worker at Eastside in Whitechapel and works with The Cable Street Group. He lives in Stepney with his partner and their two children.

Carole Satyamurti is a poet and sociologist who teaches at the University of East London. She has published a study of social work in an East London Borough, and three volumes of poetry.

Editorial

Why? Giving voice to the sub-region

RISING EAST WILL APPEAR three times a year and aims to become the leading source of information and comment on our region. The journal has its origins in a book with a similar title: *Rising in the East? The Regeneration of East London* (Lawrence and Wishart 1996). We published the book in order to bring together the fruits of various research projects being undertaken at the University of East London on the East London sub-region. At the time we had not really given much thought to the policy implications of this research programme or of longer term research needs. The university - mainly through its Single Regeneration Budget partnership bid for a new campus in the former Royal Docks - has become an important player in the regeneration strategy for the East London area. The book and the interest it has generated there created a role for the university and its academic staff in bringing together policy initiatives and research for the sub-region. One aspect of this is the successful partnership between London East Training and Enterprise Council (LETEC) and the university, one of the fruits of which is this journal.

Our intention is that, through the journal, an area with a population of several million people will acquire a voice which will promote thoughtful considerations of the issues facing the sub-region. We are under no illusions that East London will speak with one voice but hope that by encouraging people to write about the area and themselves that a regional perspective will develop which will transcend the many differences inside the area. The issues of voice and of geography are problematic, particularly in a place which has had such a long history of being spoken for and at. This journal is a positive contribution to building a relationship between the sub-region and its people, enabling us to think strategically and intelligently about the future of East London. That is our intention. What are the problems that face East London in developing its voice? The first is clearly that of geography.

The problem of geography: London and its sub-region

Geography is an issue: partly because the area is overlaid by different cultural geographies, each with their competing real and imagined demographies. We will, in forthcoming issues, explore these cultural maps and the different meanings they hold for different populations. But there is also some problem with the physical geography of the sub-region which we have defined as the eastern segment of London from Tower Bridge, including the Lee Valley area to the north, going eastwards both north and south of the Thames to include the following boroughs: Hackney, Waltham Forest, Redbridge, Tower Hamlets, Newham, Barking and Dagenham, Havering, Thurrock, Dartford, Bexley, Greenwich, Southwark and Lewisham. Some now call this London Thames Gateway or London East, but we will stick with East London until something better comes along. We will however approach the concept of geography flexibly - for instance, Drew Stevenson's approach takes in part of Haringey and Enfield.

Not surprisingly then, this is not an area that has much natural sense of cohesion split as it is into north and south by the Thames which is as big a social barrier as it is a physical one. It is also divided by poverty, class and often by ethnic and racial divisions. Nor is there any political or other institution that can speak for the area. This of course is a problem for London as a whole but, London can at least look forward to some form of urban government if the Labour Party is elected to power - to be symbolized, perhaps, by an elected mayor. This is not an option for any sub area of the city, however large it might be. East London's problems stem from its subordinate role to the rest of the city, so that if a map of London is drawn on the basis of almost any set of social and economic indicators, the east and west halves will be markedly different with the deprived half always to the east. This inequality has always been the case. The hope lies in the fact that, in recent years, East London - initially on the back of the Docklands boom - has become what is widely claimed to be the biggest regeneration project in Europe and the biggest single area of public investment in London. The concern is that mere investment of itself will change little and that is why we need a carefully crafted strategy that confronts the issues which are not merely social and economic, but which are also those of vision, culture and values. Nevertheless unless we confront the issues of economic and social deprivation of the sub-region and its inhabitants, there can be no vision for the future - only a nightmare.

A way out of the 'heads you win, tails I lose' syndrome

Why is it that East London has consistently under-performed in relation to the rest of London: is it because of failures in the London economy as a whole or is it because of the distribution of success and failure within the

London economy? There are increasingly good grounds for arguing that social deprivation is not a consequence of economic failure but of economic success - put another way, economic wealth does not 'trickle down' towards the most needy. It is almost exactly a hundred years ago since Booth surveyed every domestic property in London, research which led eventually to the welfare reforms of the early twentieth century when government finally realized that the most powerful nation on earth was rotten at its core. These reforms, which had their roots in East London, were testament to the recognition that unless attention was paid to social exclusion then economic success itself would be threatened. Nearly one hundred years later the issue of social exclusion is even more relevant: social inclusion may not follow from economic success but social exclusion will threaten sustained economic growth; that much is now becoming clear. The last twenty years show us that, far from being a prescription for economic regeneration, labour market policies which make a virtue of polarisation and pauperisation are themselves the prime threat to what remains vibrant in the London and UK economy.

Unless social issues are addressed then all the factors that have led to social exclusion in East London in the past will continue to operate. Quite simply, if nothing is done and London continues to thrive as a world city, its success will continue to be exported to the western side and to the metropolitan periphery - unless and until we put programmes in place which correct this historic tendency. If it continues to decline (in part at least because of the consequences of social exclusion such as crime and grime) then the social consequences of that economic decline will be even more focused in the east because that is where deprivation is already concentrated. Much is made of skills mismatches and the need for skilling, reskilling and upskilling, but the crucial question is who benefits from the skilling process? We have known for several decades about the 'class gradient' in education; this now appears to apply more widely to skills and employability. Research now demonstrates that it is those who are already deprived who fail to gain access to the educational and training programmes which will provide the skills and evidence of motivation that employers require. Being young, living in council or housing association accommodation, being an unmarried male, being disabled, not being white - each of these factors doubles the chances of remaining unemployed and these factors are cumulative. As Vikki Rix's analysis in the section *Trends East* shows for those who didn't already know it, these disadvantages (some social, some biological) are heavily concentrated in East London and imply a lifetime without work for many living in the sub-region. Unless we can devise policies and programmes that mesh with the needs, motivations and aspirations of people living in our region then we will go on doubling the chances of social failure until the opportunities for regeneration become infinitesimally small. We wish to make one final point on geography; it is striking that other regions in Europe have recognized the importance of the region not only in relation to national government but also to the European Community. If East London is to get the policies and investment it deserves then London *must* acquire a regional identity and East London a sub-regional identity within it: hopefully one function this journal can perform is to give voice to that sense of self identity - both to its citizens and to policy-makers in Whitehall and Brussels.

Why we need a debate

There is now a vast development programme taking place in East London and there is a chance to change the historically unbalanced way that London has developed. That process requires social policy as well as civil engineering, that much seems to be recognized; it also requires an investment of 'intellectual capital' which means creating a platform for information and debate as much as building schools and decontaminating land. Often that information or debate will not be welcome to those responsible for 'place marketing' the sub-region, but that is a cost which will have to borne. It is now widely accepted that marketing costs are a major element of production in the private sector whether in the manufacturing or services sector. The same point can be made about gaining public involvement and consent about a vision for the future and ensuring that it is implemented. Seattle, as Drew Stevenson points out, which is a city many times smaller and less complex than East London, spent millions of dollars on just the public consultation aspect of its strategic planning. This journal is one contribution to that process.

Most of us do not usually approach journals with joy; they are often a duty to be endured. This is, to a greater or lesser extent inevitable, since weighty subjects require in-depth analysis and difficult subjects cannot always be made easy. But we intend to balance the content of the journal, hence our decision to divide it into a number of sections which will overlap in terms of content and so provide different ways into issues. East London is an incredibly complex place and hopefully writing about it will give rise to imaginative ideas about making it better place in which to work, live and play. You may start at the back on the 'cultural stuff' but we hope that you will then find your way to the front, whilst those who started at the front will have their virtue rewarded by the time they reach the end.

There is no publication for those who are interested in reading about

East London, which after all is an area larger than many national capitals. National newspapers are only interested when some anarchists claim they are going to 'mug a yuppie' in Docklands and the *Evening Standard* reports disappointingly little about what happens east of Aldgate. Local papers are just that: they cannot often provide in-depth study and are usually parochial. Local authorities produce or commission good reports, as do organizations like LETEC for the sub-region as a whole, but most people do not see them. We aim to draw on these resources, our own researches in the university, and research from elsewhere. We will also, thanks to the support of LETEC, commission new writing on the sub-region.

Future issues and contents

In the next issue, Michael Rustin will continue the debate on strategy in the first section of this issue by responding to the contributions by Anna Whyatt and Drew Stevenson; looking further ahead, we will have a series of articles on 'life after the LDDC' and in particular the developments in the Royal Docks. We will be investigating how much has been learnt from the Isle of Dogs experience: do we now have an infrastructure but not much else? We will also be looking at localities within the sub-region and how they relate to it as a whole: Lee Valley, Hackney and Stratford. In forthcoming issues, we are planning two articles with a comparative perspective, one about urban regeneration in the United States and the other about Barcelona which is often seen as a European success story. We also are planning to write about the impact of the international passenger station at Stratford and, in somewhat different vein, on social exclusion studies using biographical methods and on the legacy of the various City Challenge and City Partnership programmes.

In the second section *Trends East* (which is edited by Vikki Rix from UEL), we will usually be able to relate the coverage to one or more of the major first section articles. We intend to give in depth trend analysis of health inequalities, education, family and household structure and also to crime and social justice. Each time, statistical and demographic analysis will be contextualized within a debate about current trends.

We have entitled the third section *Arty Facts*. Here we will publish shorter, more journalistic, often illustrated, articles on the cultural life of East London commissioned by Ruth Borthwick. This is not (just) meant to be light relief from the heavy stuff in sections one and two. It will provide a different way of getting oriented to what is going on in East London, recognising that cultural representations provide a basis for understanding perceptions and behaviour.

Our future plans include photo essays on a barber's shop in Stamford Hill and on Bangladeshi boys, and articles on the construction of Mile End Park, artists in East London, and a black history of Lewisham. We also hope to be able to carry an interview with Bryan Gould who was for many years the MP for Barking and Dagenham and is now living in New Zealand on his perspective on future prospects for the sub-region. We will have reviews of a recent study on regeneration programmes in Manchester and Sheffield, *A Tale of Two Cities*, and of the recent Museum of London exhibition on Chinese women in Limehouse, for example. We will also include, given the constraints imposed by long lead times, notice of important forthcoming events. If you would like to contribute details of your event, please note the addresses at the front of the journal.

This issue

We lead this issue with *Structuring Change in the Sub-region: values, vision and governance in East London*. Its author is Drew Stevenson, who was appointed to the LDDC chair of Urban Regeneration during 1996 with the specific task of developing a regeneration strategy for the East London sub-region. This article represents his initial thinking about this strategy and also serves, in part at least, as a manifesto for the journal and in raising issues for debate. His approach in developing this strategy puts a lot of the emphasis on developing a vision which needs to reflect the values of those living in the sub-region. Taken with Anna Whyatt's article, *Thames Gateway London in the Millennium* which proposes an ambitious economic development strategy, these two articles are intended to put forward proposals which can give an indication of a way forward. Anna Whyatt argues that the future of the sub-region lies in developing an economic strategy which is tied into the economy of the London region. The Thames Gateway London sub-region must develop a 'leading edge' role in retailing, producer services, business and financial services, manufacturing, gateway/logistics, printing and tourism. This will all require a heavy investment in skills. She sees the sub-region as perched precariously between a circle of decline and one of prosperity. The essential need is for the Thames Gateway to act in cohort with a strategy for engaging the future.

The three other articles that comprise the first section are very different but all engage with major issues. Rob Home's *Building a Mosque in Stepney: ethnic minorities and the planning system* is a study of the attempt by part of the Muslim community in Tower Hamlets, where it makes up nearly a quarter of the population, to build a mosque. His study of the obstruction they faced from the planning regulations and what he sees as the council's over-sensitivity to the feelings of other residents about the idea of a visible mosque, highlights the need to recognize that East London's future will depend on the needs and strengths of a diverse group of cultures. The fact that many of the Asian communities of East London are amongst the most entrepreneurial needs to be recognized, if we are not to lose them from the sub-region once they have achieved economic success. Too often in the past, this has been the history of such groups. In contrast, Caroline Knowles's *Race and Place in 'Schizophrenic' Narratives* shows how black activists have managed to reorganize parts at least of the community mental health system in East London and have created several black centres devoted to meeting the needs of black people diagnosed as mentally ill. She shows how this has become a complex medley of provision in which black patients often visit a number of centres or else choose one that meets their particular definitions of themselves. She concludes that despite the success of black people in 'racializing community space', this has been limited by the organization of the system which 'works against the needs of its users'. She suggests that more fundamental and racially articulate reforms are necessary to address the needs of those forced to use the system. Margaret O'Brien's and Deborah Jones's article *Young People, Family Life and Education in Barking and Dagenham: three case studies* is an examination of family life particularly in relation to education. They have revisited one of the localities investigated by Peter Willmott in the 1950s - Barking and Dagenham - but from the vantage point of the 1990s with all its particular preoccupations, some of which are not so far from those of the 1950s. Their findings indicate a fascinating blend of continuity and change: the family still maintains a very close pull especially on young female workers and girls, getting experience of work is still valued far more than gaining education qualifications despite the fact that the area has a low rate of unemployment, and household incomes are higher than elsewhere in East London. Nevertheless for those concerned with upskilling the new generation, the findings must be of concern.

We have entitled our second section *Trends East* and in this first issue, Vikki Rix looks at the latest labour market trends in the sub-region and the data that she provides here provides a sombre backdrop for the two lead articles by Stevenson and Whyatt. She shows that our sub-region's population is one which is relatively deprived compared to the rest of London in terms of prospects and advantage. She also shows that there has been an increase in social exclusion and socio-economic polarisation. There are interesting differences within the region particularly between the inner and outer areas and, to a lesser extent, between those areas to the north and south of the river.

What is it that makes an East End novel 'East End'? Ken Worpole's search for the answer to this tricky question leads him to some fascinating conclusions in *The Talking Cure: Harold Pinter and the voices of East End writers*, the first article to kick off *Arty Facts*, our focus on cultural life east of Hampstead. Using Michael Billington's recent biography as a way of reading Harold Pinter, probably the most successful writer to emerge from East London, Ken Worpole suggests that Pinter's work must be seen as part of a rich body of literature which has its roots in the culture of East End institutions and meeting places.

If the words tourism and East London seem unlikely adjuncts to you, then Bruce Jerram and Richard Wells aim to change all that. In *Having a Wonderful Time: on developing a visitor economy for East London*, the authors argue that developing a tourist economy for the sub-region is crucial not only to its own development, but to that of the whole of London. Noting examples from overseas of other cities with similar post-industrial legacies, such as derelict sites and contaminated ground, they propose a tourism which has uppermost in its strategy, improvement for local people as well as for adventurous visitors. This is the opening salvo in a debate on a controversial industry for the sub-region which we shall be pursuing in future issues.

In *The Art of Cable Street*, Roger Mills commemorates the sixtieth anniversary of the Battle of Cable Street, arguably the heaviest defeat of fascism in Britain by the combined left. Roger Mills argues that it is the Battle's unique position as a success of the British left unblemished by sectarian conflict which has led to its wide depiction in a spectrum of art forms from the spectacular mural at the site to musical and theatrical representations which resonate with life today.

Finally, Carole Satyamurti reviews a new book written by a researcher long associated with the sub-region, Michael Young. *A Good Death* concerns itself with people dying in St. Joseph's Hospice in Hackney, a major East End institution. The book is a powerful intervention in the debate about the need for a dignified death and should be noted by the living.

Please do let us know what you think about the journal, what you would like to see in it and if you would like to write for it - our address is inside the front cover.

Welcome to *Rising East*!

Tim Butler

Structuring change in the sub-region:

Values, Vision and Governance in East London

Drew Stevenson

Drew Stevenson's paper looks at some fundamental questions concerning London's future. He argues that transformational change will not happen without a clear long-term strategy that is developed with a wide range of partners and implemented over at least a 15 year period. Controversially, he argues that the strategy must be vision-led rather than trend-led and must be based on the emerging values held by young people if it is to remain relevant over the period of its implementation.

IN THIS ARTICLE I want to explore a number of issues relating to the construction of strategies for the regeneration of East London - see Map 1.

East London Regeneration Area

First, I want to look at the context in which any regeneration strategy has to be prepared. In particular I shall argue that in order to stand any chance of relevance, let alone success, strategy has to be vision-led rather than trend-led. And I shall argue that the construction of a relevant vision has in turn to be based on an understanding of significant shifts in values held by Londoners between different generations. It is the value set of the young that will, given the long lead-in times of major regeneration, hold sway over the majority of the period of implementation of any longer term strategy devised today.

Second, I want to outline those elements which, in my view, a strategy for the regeneration of East London should cover - and I will suggest the broad content of each element. The emphasis is on those actions which will lead not just to change, but to transformation.

Finally, I shall briefly look at the process by which such a strategy could be prepared and implemented, based upon the various proposals and partnerships that already exist. Without a broadly-based sense of ownership and a range of partnerships committed to implementation, it will never materialise. These issues will take us into the realm of governance and legitimacy.

Do we need a strategy?

Is a strategy really needed and if so, why? This question takes many forms, many of which imply a negative answer. 'Surely not another strategy?' Or 'Is it really sensible to have a plan for this part of London alone?' Or 'Don't we want action now instead of more talk and plans?' This sense of exasperation is understandable. It is often held by those who are genuinely anxious to see some action to improve conditions and life in the UK's most deprived sub-region. It is born both of disappointment in the results of previous plan-making and in the sheer scale of the problem. To do something, anything, is seen as better than doing nothing.

It is paradoxical that the impatience with strategic planning currently lies largely within the public sector whilst the private sector, now used to the rigours of longer term thinking in their own organisations, has reversed its previous hostility to such planning. Meanwhile central government increasingly demands that large bids for competitive funding are set in some kind of regional context, yet falls far short of embracing the notion of a regional or sub-regional strategy. It has to be said that this stance by government is not only illogical, but it carries within it the seeds of auto-destruction. How is it possible to run a Regional Challenge competition with no acknowledged notion of what the regional regeneration strategy is, nor how any received bids may contribute to, or conversely undermine, such a strategy?

There is undoubtedly political opposition to regional strategies, since they lead to demands for regional governments to oversee their implementation (in the spirit of subsidiarity) - a concept which the Government relentlessly opposes. But there is no easy way out, since the current arrangements lead to judgements on major publicly funded schemes being made either without any concept as to how they will, or won't, benefit the priority needs of a region - or there is in fact a regional strategy that has been constructed without consultation and remains opaque. Neither position, I suggest, is sustainable in the longer term. I make this point because it illustrates very clearly the need for someone to have a view about the priorities for investment in a region and the issues of governance that underlie it.

The arguments for having regional strategies run deep. First, in a very real sense the late 1990s can be characterised as the age of the region and, within that, the concept of sub-regions is gaining importance. Why? Because at the European Union (EU) level work is increasingly being done on the delineation of new super regions - the Euro regions. For example London and South-East England are being seen as part of the Euro region of the 'Central Capital Cities' - a region of some 50 million people encompassing London, Paris, Bonn, the Randstad and Brussels. The significance of this for smaller regions lies partly in the impact on intellectual thought of such large organisational concepts. It means in practice that serious debate about very large geographic areas is making it far easier to grasp some of the issues affecting sub-regions the size of East London. An area that once seemed impossibly large and hugely diverse now seems positively compact and fairly homogenous. At the very least the sub-region's diversity can now more easily be seen as an aspect of its functional totality, rather than as a set of unrelated and unintelligible social, economic and spatial variables.

The second argument for having regional strategies follows the first - namely that large scale public sector money, be it EU or UK government, is increasingly accessible *only* at the regional or sub-regional level. Within the UK this is causing a number of problems. With a tradition of anti-regionalism developed over the past 20 years or so (which coincides with the period when the EU concept has become established) we are left with no democratic or effective political institutions at the regional level, particularly in London and the south-east. Nor do we have co-ordinated databases, nor participative frameworks. It may or may not be an intentional consequence of European regionalism to undermine the UK's access to EU money in this way. But there is now a major imperative to sort out our regions and develop the mechanisms for deciding on their role within the national economy and on their relevance to EU funding streams.

A further consequence of this anti-regionalism is that the UK now has to rely on partnerships to forge a view of regional futures since the political mechanisms are not there. It could be argued that this was no bad thing in that it gives an added incentive for partnerships to form and gel. In practice it is not that simple and the resultant difficulties in agreeing strategy and the accompanying strains on governance will be returned to later in this paper.

Third - there are growing demands for clarity and transparency about the future of cities and regions, and there is a growing number of global role models which illustrate the dramatic impact that a clear sense of vision can have - Barcelona, Seattle and Curitiba for example, or closer to home, Glasgow. The transformation of these cities has *not* happened by accident, or by good fortune - or overnight. It has occurred because someone with political power (and the skill to negotiate a broadly based consensus) developed a vision for the future of the city and remained in power long enough to ensure its implementation - usually about 15 years. The construction and ownership of strategy was the key. To quote Pascal Maragall, Mayor of Barcelona for the past 14 years, 'Barcelona knew how to make a good analysis and to build good projects. We analysed our assets and liabilities, what we have and what we lack, and this formed the basis for our long term plan, which is to transform the city in co-operation with employers, unions, our citizens, the universities and the chamber of commerce, positioning it in the forefront of the new Europe. Having a strategy is the most important thing' (*The Independent*, 29 October 1996).

These three reasons for developing regional or sub-regional strategies - European regionalism, accessing competitive funding on a large scale, and the need for clarity and transparency - have a particular impact on London.

When looking at London's economic development, the 32 borough boundaries do not make sense. Given the fact that there is no strategic London-wide authority, it is a somewhat abstract argument to consider whether or not a London-wide strategy on its own would be enough - that is to say without the addition of sub-regional strategies within London. Nonetheless I would argue strongly that *in the context* of a London-wide strategy, sub-regional strategies within London are necessary to clarify the complimentary functions of the sub-regions, to inform the construction of the city-wide strategy and to ensure its relevant local implementation. The reasons for this relate to the sheer size and complexity of London. Compared to other European Union cities that have city-wide strategies, London with a population of 6.8m is very big. Paris is 2.4m, Frankfurt 660 thousand, Barcelona 1.6 million etc. London is also extremely diverse - culturally, racially and economically.

Increasingly the view is being taken that London contains three major identifiable sub-regions: West London, Central London and East London. This is not to deny that other meaningful agglomerations of communities and activities make sense at a geographic level and that many valid partnerships exist to reflect those areas. But the three sub-regions of West, Central, East are of a different scale and economic impact (whatever arguments there may be over their exact boundaries).

Central London as the seat of government, headquarters functions, finance and business services, historic spaces and buildings as well as tourist-related activities remains the pre-eminent sub-region in London. But it does not and cannot stand alone. West London provides major infrastructure and research establishments, the IT corridor to the West and a dynamic industrial complex at Park Royal.

East London completes the sub-regional picture. For the purposes of this article I am referring to the area shown on Map 1 characterised by rapidly improving infrastructure, massive development site opportunities, an entrepreneurial tradition and over a third of London's manufacturing capacity. It is shortly to be connected directly to continental Europe with a station on the Channel Tunnel Rail Link (CTRL) at Stratford. It possesses its own short take-off and landing (STOL) airport in the Royal Docks and it will host the Millennium Festival on the Greenwich peninsula.

These are London's pre-eminent sub-regions. And yet there is a worrying difference between them. Central London is characterised by comparatively great economic security and has recently acquired a new partnership which is examining the linkages between the centre and its hinterlands, particularly the South Bank. West London has had a major partnership in existence for some years and has just released a radical and forward thinking document for the future of the sub-region (*West London Leadership* 1996). In East London we have some catching up to do. Whilst arguably London's future and potential lies here in the East and a great deal of excellent work is being done across the sub-region, we have neither the partnership mechanism nor the strategy to release and realise that potential. This essay proposes some critical steps that need to be faced to rectify this position.

Constructing the strategy

There are two classic approaches to strategy-making. One is to project existing trends and to try to analyse where they will make problems worse, or create new problems and attempt to devise a strategy to deal with them. It is a familiar and apparently attractive process. Attractive because it is held to be founded on 'reality' - the projection of real facts and figures; it deals with clearly identified problems - the solution to which could make a real difference; and it is consensus-building in that it is comparatively easy to cement a body of opinion around the problems that are to be addressed. If used in isolation however there are some real problems. The projection of trends is only possible where data exists over a period of time; the implication of this is that one is really looking backwards not forwards. Secondly, projection is simply not a sensible way of looking to the future. The future is never a straight-line projection from the past. A more sophisticated method is to introduce an element of prediction, but this brings the use of judgement into play and hence the basis of 'certainty' and consensus begins to evaporate.

The simple use of projections or predictions is also to misunderstand the cause and nature of change. If we attempt a prediction, we can only do it with any sense of probability if it relates to a situation over which we have some control or to a relatively closed system where we have expert and detailed knowledge. We therefore tend to predict changes, say to a business, that relate to potential changes in our market, or income streams and so on. Whilst these are important they remain internal and the really big changes that make or break businesses are almost always external and unforeseen. It is not so much that they are beyond our sphere of influence (although they often are) but that they are beyond our sphere of *looking*.

There are other techniques which are being developed to try and anticipate change - see for example the 'Serious Futures' model developed by Demos, Perri 6 (1996) Annex 2. This model attempts to assess the vulnerability of key 'internal' factors, such as production streams, to external change - and then looks at which of those are more or less likely to happen and whether they would have a major impact or not. The idea being to guard against a range of possible futures and be poised to seize new positive opportunities as they arise.

Amongst those 'external' changes I would argue that shifts in the values held by UK society are amongst the most critical when preparing a strategy not just for a business but for the capital city. The reason for this is that any strategy for the future of London has to be about influencing change and not just reacting to it. There is no point in projecting or even predicting the future and then devising a strategy designed to make it happen - since your projection is that it will happen anyway. Strategies need to start from a clear analysis of what we want to change as well as the direction in which we wish to change. Both of these ultimately relate to the set of values held by society.

Without a set of values, explicit or implicit, against which some aspect of the status quo clashes, we would see no reason to change that status quo.

The problem is that the values held by any society themselves change over time. Why is this and what are the implications for strategy-making? There are several drivers of changes in values over the past fifty years, the most important in the UK being increasing education, communication and travel combined with a period of freedom from global warfare and of economic growth and social change - particularly the role of women (Wilkinson 1996). These have impacted on values held in the UK such that the value sets held by different generations have shifted. Contrary to popular belief, values held by individuals do not change greatly over their lifetime. Significantly, people do not tend to develop a set of more conservative values (arguably more akin to their parents) as they age. Instead each generation tends to form a set of values between the ages 18 - 24 which they then carry with them largely unaltered through life (Wilkinson and Mulgen 1995). And there is a pattern to this change across generations.

Whilst there is a set of 'core' values that are broadly shared by most in society, there is a distinct shift in emphasis in the values beyond the 'core' held by the young and the elderly. Crudely put, those people who formed their values fifty years ago lean towards a set of values that emphasise the family, puritanism, rigidity and the rule of law. Conversely today's young people tend to emphasise living life on the edge, a blurring of 'male' and 'female' roles, welcoming internationalism and a sense of inter-connectedness (Wilkinson and Mulgen 1995). Whilst it is true that there are some differences between social groups, the general direction of change is remarkably consistent, as Helen Wilkinson puts it 'generation is becoming a better predictor of attitudes than class or geography' (Wilkinson 1996). In her book *No Turning Back*, she also demonstrates that the values held by men and women are converging at a dramatic rate, with the changes in values held by women leading the way. There is regrettably however, given the nature of the data available over time, little information on the values held by minority ethnic groups. The most that can be inferred from existing sources is that there is a shift to far greater tolerance of difference and an acceptance of the rights of others and that this appears to be driven by generation rather than other social factors.

There is also evidence that these 'new' values are the 'leading edge' values and as time goes by the values of each new young generation shift to become the core values of society as a whole, whereas the values of older people become more and more peripheral, being held by fewer people.

Two final points in this short sketch of UK values; first there is some evidence that these 'leading edge' values are more widely held in the UK than in other countries (Demos, forthcoming). Second some current work being done by the London Planning and Advisory Committee (LPAC) in association with Demos and the London Arts Board suggests that these same values are far more widely held in London than elsewhere in the UK and that the trailing edge values are disappearing in London at a faster rate than elsewhere (LPAC, forthcoming).

So what does this tell us about strategy development in London? There is a sense in which London is at the forefront globally in that Londoners hold a set of values that will become increasingly commonplace across all major cities worldwide. London is where it is 'at' if you are young and forward looking: it is the place to be. It feels, and is, sympathetic to young attitudes and provides opportunities for networking as well as a sense of 'belonging' to a range of non-geographically based communities.

However, it is not the purpose of this paper to propose a motivating vision for London, indeed there are very real concerns as to whether a single theme can ever encompass a description of London in our increasingly complex and fast changing society. But there are some pointers. Just as Anna Whyatt's paper elsewhere suggests certain key economic roles and sectors that London should play, so I would argue that London needs to promote itself in some way as facilitating creativity, celebrating cultural diversity and enabling people to live the kinds of lives they want to lead, rather than imposing a set of roles upon them. And there is a clear sense that a future strategy must relate to the values of the young if it is to be meaningful. By the time the vision is made reality it will be their values that form the core values held by most Londoners.

I am not suggesting here that these values have been created in the abstract - free from influences of the market and the constraints of individual powerlessness. (It is however interesting to note that the values are moving in a direction opposite to what might have been predicted after 17 years of national conservatism at the political level.) Nor am I suggesting that they are inherently good - or bad. I am merely saying that policy makers ignore them at their peril. As Helen Wilkinson brilliantly puts it 'Over the medium term institutions have a simple choice: they can either rethink their values and adapt to change or they can be rendered irrelevant by it' (Wilkinson 1996).

What else will affect the construction of a vision? Without diverting from my main thesis that a strategy for London's future must be primarily vision-led rather than trend-led, there are certain arenas of change that must be acknowledged. These major changes are 'external' changes over which we in London will have little direct control. It is important however to understand them and to position our vision in a manner that goes with the grain of these changes or is as robust as possible against them where necessary. The key issue is how to guide the direction of change, with what effect, with what outcomes and for whom.

These changes are fivefold.

First, very much linked to the changes in values referred to above, we are witnessing a radical change in ethos which will fundamentally alter our perception of the city. This change has been described as a shift from a culture of dependence (the welfare state) to independence (the Thatcher years) to interdependence (Frye 1996). Within this shift, integration and inclusivity are becoming the dominant concepts of societal organisation. Interestingly, this shift is not being led solely, if at all, by major political movements or a moral crusade. It is led by a growing pragmatic realisation that, in an age of information exchange, organisations or institutions simply cannot survive independently. The move by large scale business towards out-sourcing epitomises this shift; together with their consequent interdependence on a range of small just-in-time suppliers, it is altering perceptions about desirable models of societal organisation.

Second, these new models carry the need to re-examine and reform relationships. The ways in which people, groups and businesses relate to one another are changing and the new interest in this is in turn reflected in the leading edge values held by the young. It is here that the fundamental shift from an interest in green issues to the dominant concept of sustainability has taken root. There is a growing sense that if the future is not sustainable, socially, economically and environmentally, there will not be a future at all. Sustainability is now at the core of the agenda determining urban affairs.

Third, partnership as a concept is interwoven with changes in values, ethos and relationships, but deserves separate mention because of the possibilities for joint social action that have not existed before. But the new partnerships, extending as they do over geographic areas which do not conform to local authority boundaries raise critical issues of governance. I will return to these at the end of this article.

Fourth, and turning more to East London, there are changes relating to the structural position of East London both within the European context and within London that will impact on future visions. East London will shortly have an international passenger station on the high speed rail network that connects Europe's capital and major cities. Setting aside for a moment the significance of the station, the impact of the network itself will alter the psychological concept of London's proximity to other European cities. Take, for example, our concept of where Paris lies in relation to London. For the past 15 years it has taken two hours to travel to York by train and, until a year ago, about seven hours to travel to Paris by train. Psychologically this put Paris about 3½ times further away than York (instead of approximately the same distance) - that means Paris was somewhere on the edge of the Mediterranean on our psychological map. Now it is possible to leave Marseilles at breakfast time by train and have a late lunch in London.

Finally, there will be the impact of the Millennium. Not only is the site of the festival located here in the eastern part of London, but the Lottery fund is opening up funding required to help realise previously impossible schemes. But most of all the Millennium is creating a shift in expectation, optimism and determination. There is a demand for a new and better future than that handed down in East London over the past 200 years.

To summarise: whether we plan for it or not, change will come to East London. It will be driven largely by the unexpected and by forces beyond our direct control. But we can anticipate some of these forces for change and we can seek to influence their direction, their impact and their outcomes. We cannot however seek to do that unless we have a clear and shared vision of what we want East London to become, and unless we relate that vision to a set of emerging values which will make it appropriate to the period of its implementation.

Towards a regeneration strategy for East London

In that context I want to turn to the elements that I believe a regeneration strategy should contain before moving on in the final section to look briefly at the process for producing the strategy.

It seems to me that there should be five elements to a regeneration strategy for the sub-region of East London, they are:

- economic
- social
- infrastructural
- environmental
- developmental

These five elements overlap and are linked by shifts in values, changes in relationships, by sustainability, and by a determination to effect change, challenge the status quo, change image and expectations and harness the potential of all in this most culturally and racially diverse sub-region of the most diverse city in the world. Two other elements are strong candidates for inclusion, one is culture and the other is Europe. I have not suggested them at this stage however as I suspect they may be better treated, like equality of opportunity and sustainability, as strands which run through all of the elements rather than separate elements in themselves. Consultation will decide whether or not this is correct.

In looking at the possible content of each element, I have been conscious that until now more emphasis has perhaps been given to the 'inner city' parts of the sub-region. It is of course correct that action and resources are desperately needed in those areas; but they are needed elsewhere too and a strategy must be relevant to the whole sub-region. I have also been conscious that the real challenge is not merely about change - it is about the ability to transform the sub-region.

Economic

The economic section of any regeneration strategy for East London will clearly flow from the work done by Anna Whyatt and her colleagues, as described elsewhere in this journal. I won't repeat the arguments here, nor add to their proposals for building upon those sectors displaying most potential for growth and those relevant to the key roles and functions of the London economy. Within that context there are a few points to be made.

Developments already agreed. First, a comprehensive regeneration strategy needs to look carefully at the sub-regional impact of major developments that are already agreed. By way of illustration, there are the International Passenger Station at Stratford, the Millennium Festival development on the Greenwich peninsula, the development of the north side of the Royal Docks with the new University of East London campus and technology park and the Barking Reach site. Many other sites could be listed, such as the Lee Valley Science Park and developments at Tottenham Hale and in the Edmonton Opportunity Area.

The issues presented by these developments vary. At Stratford there is still a major question as to what will be built and how it will relate to or transform the local economy. For the Millennium Festival site the critical issues, apart from transportation, are the impact on the local economy during construction and during the festival - but also the relevance of after-uses to the sub-region and its sustainable future.

As far as the Royal Docks are concerned, critical work is continuing on the function of the campus to meet local education and skills need and to provide the support needed by existing or incoming businesses. It is important to learn lessons from continental Europe where there is a much closer working relationship between universities and the innovative capacity (in projects and in management) of business. Discussions are also continuing on the location of the Exhibition Centre here which would have a huge impact, producing a very broad range of jobs. Barking Reach is significant not only in the range and scale of housing it will provide, but in its impact on the future demand for housing land (see also below). But the strategy also needs to analyse the threats, and opportunities, of external developments, be they Terminal 5, Ebbsfleet or the potentially interesting agreed expansion of Stansted and the implications for jobs and sectors in the Stratford, Tottenham Hale, Stansted and Cambridge corridor.

Support services. Second, and complementary to the strategy to develop key sectors, further work needs to be done on analysing the role of 'non-global' industries and support services in the sub-region. The sub-region generates a large demand for products and services of all kinds. There is scope for meeting some of these demands more locally, supporting SMEs to complete successfully in terms of location and distribution costs.

Clustering. Third, there is scope to achieve a far better 'fit' between SMEs and their clustering around large companies, particularly Fords, to provide a 'just-in-time' service. A new joint initiative with Fords on this would be welcome.

Minority ethnic businesses. Fourth, building on existing initiatives, more needs to be done to 'mainstream' minority ethnic businesses, actively seeking to expand international trading links appropriate to different communities. This is a key issue to which I will return below.

A rationalisation of business support services is also needed. Experience elsewhere, e.g. Sunderland, Wigan, Birmingham, shows that the co-location and integration of TECs, Business Links, Chambers of Commerce, local authority regeneration teams and University researchers has given a dramatic new form and scope to support services. This is particularly true where they are physically combined with a Business Innovation Centre (BIC) that is actively encouraging the creation and support of new technology businesses. A network of technology parks linked to support services and a regional BIC would bring major benefits to the sub-region. The excellent work being done by the Lee Valley BIC is an encouraging start.

Information technology. The sub-region - like the UK as a whole - is lagging behind competitors on the penetration of high quality IT and business management training. This needs to be integrated with other programmes, such as IIP, and a range of funding regimes to turn the position round as fast as possible.

The labour market. Finally, as widely acknowledged, better data and a resultant strategy is needed on the labour market. That work also needs to test the impact of the new transport links - particularly the introduction of fast commuter trains from north Kent on the high speed rail link to Stratford. The ability to tap this labour force, together with that of much of East Anglia and Essex has potentially enormous implications for business location.

Social

There is a clear overlap between strategies designed to affect the sub-regional economy and those tackling the major social issues of poverty and discrimination. In a society where the Welfare State has been dismantled or undermined piece by piece, the route out of poverty for many people lies in access not just to work, but to a decent job with a reasonable wage. And therein lies the problem.

Access to, and exclusion from, work. There have recently been many conferences and papers on this subject - too broad ranging to be included in this paper. (See for example the papers from the conference on Exclusion from Work, organised by LEPU, November 1996.) The main priority for the sub-region I believe is a review of the vast range of initiatives being taken internationally and to reach a view on which actions are likely to be most relevant to the sub-region, based on those that will attack causes rather than effects and those that are people-centred and locally deliverable. Some will be short-term, some longer-term and many will only be capable of implementation at a supra-regional level. I am not suggesting that such a package will bring an end to unemployment in East London, but I believe we could be far clearer on a range of actions than we currently are. A cross-sector task force to look at this would be a helpful start, and a fundamental part of developing a relevant sub-regional regeneration strategy. The starting point has to be the provision of knowledge and skills relevant to the jobs available now and in the future.

Target training. The traditional approach of targeting training by geography or by sector needs to be broadened to deal directly with exclusion in terms of minority ethnic exclusion and exclusion on ground of gender, disability and age.

Set new EU priorities. Given the enormous racial diversity of East London, there is a strong case for trying to get the European Commission to set new priorities for dealing with such exclusion here. It needs to become a key goal for the wider transformation of the sub-region and to affect the impact of funding regimes.

New bids. With or without those new priorities more radical schemes need to be put forward for EU and SRB funding that deal directly with exclusion. A range of flagship schemes should be developed as a matter of priority in close consultation with the communities concerned and involving the voluntary sector.

New patterns of working. The shift from full-time to part-time work and the dismantling of employment safeguards has rightly been criticised. But given its wide impact there is a danger of over-looking the relevance of part-time work to many in the community who, for a variety of reasons, cannot work or do not wish to work full-time. Their rights to support and representation need addressing in a more constructive manner.

People-based priorities. It is often said that there is a shortage of jobs but not a shortage of work to be done. This is particularly true in the 'people-based' or caring aspects of work. This issue can only be addressed by a transformation of the values and ethos of society with a commitment to pay for things that are considered too expensive in a market dominated economy. Clearly such a transformation cannot happen at the sub-regional level, but the delineation and funding of innovative projects in defined areas could help demonstrate the wider benefit of new approaches. There is no reason why East London should not seek to take the lead in this arena which will become one of the key issues facing society in the new millennium.

Infrastructure

There are four potential areas of action outlined here.

Building upon recent change. The combination of the Jubilee Line Extension, the regeneration of the Docklands and its increasing occupation, the decision to build an International Passenger Station at Stratford and the Millennium Festival on the Greenwich peninsula are already giving a new profile to the sub-region. But the actual impact is lagging far behind the potential impact of such dramatic developments. Closer working with English Partnerships and the London First Centre based around a clearer view of sub-regional priorities would seem an important early step.

New infrastructure priorities. Looking to future infrastructure investment, there is a need to get agreement between the communities and all major partners on the priorities for future infrastructure in the sub-region. If that sounds difficult, it must be remembered that just such an exercise was carried out successfully London-wide through the London Pride partnership.

Infrastructure and the development of key centres. One of the implications of sustainability is the need to locate new development close to public transport and yet close enough to the homes of those who can only work part-time and therefore who have the least time available for travel. The implications of this are discussed under 'development' below.

Communication networks and new technologies. Infrastructure is not just about provision for the movement of people, but spans communication networks, including new technologies. The importance of this is increasingly acknowledged in the sub-region with, for example, some interesting telematics projects being funded under Objective 2. Nonetheless there remains an alarming complacency about the importance of new technology amongst East London firms and this will remain an important strand of any strategy (London East TEC 1996).

Environment

Much has been written about the history of environmental degradation in East London and the legacy of pollution and ill health left in its wake (Butler and Rustin 1996). I take it as read that a sub-regional strategy will give a high priority to environmental quality. Within that context I would highlight the need for two other matters to be included in the environmental section of the strategy.

New opportunities. Any serious programme for tackling this legacy of pollution will produce opportunities for jobs as well as for an improved environment.

Given the international concern over green issues any innovative solutions developed here would be highly exportable. Thus we should look at our problem of pollution also as an opportunity for the creation of new technologies, products, jobs and export potential. The development of the 'London Pride Waste Action Programme' is a good example of the kind of initiative that would be particularly relevant in East London.

Building image and confidence. Such an approach also links directly with improving image and building confidence. Specific projects need to be designed which deal with visible environmental problems (undergrounding the power lines for example) as well as invisible aspects of the contamination of land. The spin-off will not just be in the marketing of the sub-region but in very real improved health conditions.

Development

Last but not least in the areas to be covered by the strategy is development. Until a few years ago development may well have been seen as the key, if not only, element of a regeneration strategy. Most development policies however deal at a more local level than the sub-region; I want to concentrate on four issues which need to be addressed sub-regionally.

Land supply. One of the key attractions of the sub-region is its supply of large and attractive sites - not necessarily all available for immediate development. These opportunities are distributed fairly evenly through the Thames Gateway part of the region, north and south of the river: Stratford, the Royal Docks, Barking Creek, Rainham, Havering Dockside, Erith, Dartford, The Woolwich Arsenal, The Greenwich Peninsula and so on. Within the Lee Valley area, again there is a fairly wide spread, partly in the Lower Lee but mostly to the north in Tottenham, Edmonton and Enfield with improved links to the M25.

The issue is not a shortage of sites, but an over-supply. That is why the concept of a Western and Eastern Focus for development as set out in the 'Thames Gateway Planning Framework' (Department of the Environment 1995) is helpful. A similar approach is being taken in the Lee Valley. This concept of nodes or centres of particular accessibility and attraction is vital if development is to be sustainable and make an impact on the image of the sub-region. To the development industry it provides clarity; to the authorities it should help to avoid wasteful and very expensive competition for a comparatively limited amount of potential development.

Phasing and interim uses. This over-supply of land raises the issue of phasing and suitable interim uses or upgrading.

Some of the sites that are best located from a sustainable point of view are also those that carry a development cost due to pollution. In some cases the advantages of the location produce an added value that enables the clearance of pollutants, still leaving a commercially viable development. In other cases it does not. There will therefore have to be a resolution of the tension between carrying out development on 'cheaper' but less well located sites from the point of view of sustainability, and developing the more appropriate sites (thereby also dealing in many cases with environmental 'eyesores') at highly visible locations in the sub-region.

There is also the impact on the image of the sub-region of those sites which will remain undeveloped for many years. Money will have to be allocated in any regeneration package for at least the visual improvement of key sites - for example the possible provision of landscaping and temporary leisure/open space use.

Flagship projects. It has become fashionable to talk of flagship projects - and it is now becoming equally fashionable to criticise them as attracting too much attention while other issues remain unresolved.

Only the consultation process on a regeneration strategy for East London can resolve how the issue is perceived here. My own view is that flagships are important as part of a far wider package, but *only if* they are relevant to the sub-region itself *and* are related clearly to other strands of the strategy.

Thus in East London, to reflect the cultural diversity, the legacy of pollution and poor health, the industrial heritage and aspirations for the future, a number of potential projects suggest themselves.

- An Asian Cultural and Arts Centre
  (like the Institute du Monde Arabe in Paris)
- A Museum of Medicine and Health
- A Centre for Art and New Technology
- A Museum of Industrial Heritage

The list could be much longer and will need to be developed to include relevant flagships in the outer parts of the area. The list is intended to convey a feeling for the kinds of projects which would meet the criteria listed above, be of interest to local people and help secure the development of tourism as a key sector.

Quality. Finally, the strategy needs to be clear on its aspirations for quality developments. As in many elements of the strategy, this is controversial and difficult to achieve. Some would argue that it is better to secure development of any sort and thereby create jobs rather than hold out for higher quality, and therefore increase cost.

But this is to polarise the issue and it ignores the fact that there are many cases of higher environmental quality leading to a competitive edge. An obvious example of this is the construction of superstores over the past decade. They have moved from being sheds to the sophistication (albeit not in all cases) of good design by the country's leading architects.

I believe that the strategy must never lose sight of the importance of tackling the issue of poor image and environmental quality head-on if it is to succeed. Without it transformation will not occur.

How to prepare the strategy?

This question is as big again as the earlier questions addressed in this article on 'why have a strategy?' and 'what should it contain?' It warrants a separate article - not least because it raises very difficult questions of genuine participation and of governance at the sub-regional level. I will conclude this article therefore by giving only a flavour of some of the issues involved. The context for all that follows is that the strategy needs to be built upon the many excellent ideas, proposals and plans that exist. It is about co-ordination, the elimination of overlap and conflict, the identification of gaps and about a uniting vision that has transformational capacity.

Ownership. The question of ownership of strategy is inseparable from questions of leadership, governance and implementation. Where is the vision going to come from, who has the legitimacy to provide it, who will be able to ensure implementation, over what period and with what accountability? These are all major questions that are very difficult to answer at present in the UK sub-regions. Briefly put, the reasons for this difficulty have to do with a new set of issues that are beginning to dominate local governance. There are five strands to this.

First, the growing relevance of the sub-region as an arena for economic and hence social change itself poses problems. It is a geography that is not familiar to local government, nor are the institutions, structures or data in place to secure leadership and vision at this level.

Second, the growth in partnerships is changing the climate in which governance sits. Partnerships used to support local government (for instance school compacts) on a single issue; they now often cover more complex issues on a neighbourhood basis involving decision-making structures where local government is in the minority (City Challenge). Most recently they cover wide geographic areas (often driven by competitive funding regimes) seeking to knit together a large range of interests that no longer conform to local government boundaries at all.

Third, access to large-scale regeneration funds is itself becoming more remote from local governance of any kind. Gone are the days when local access to segmented main line programmes was more or less guaranteed, based (for all its imperfections) on a system of allocation by need. In its place are systems whose objectives are determined at arms length by the UK government or in Brussels, accessed not by need but by competition for integrated funding regimes. Other institutions, notably TECs, have direct access to these funds, thus further undermining the assumed legitimacy of local government leadership.

Fourth, just as local authorities were grappling locally to put in place genuine participation and a more democratic approach to service delivery, the focus is switching to the sub-region and no one has yet achieved meaningful citizen participation (or even the proper involvement of the voluntary sector) at this scale.

Finally, in the midst of all of this, local government itself is struggling to switch from operational structures designed to manage the in-house delivery of services to outward looking structures appropriate to regeneration, development and promotion.

These five issues are leading to a damaging confusion over the legacy of the past, new forms of leadership and legitimacy and the ability to construct (let alone hold together) a vision and delivery mechanism for the sustainable future of the new sub-regions. These are extraordinarily difficult issues to resolve. They affect not just East London, but sub-regions across the country.

Partnership, participation and genuine joint working. The only way forward is to develop further the concepts and mutual trust inherent in *genuine* partnership working. Again, this is not easy: it is perhaps only the realisation that to fail to do so puts the future of the sub-region at risk that will make it happen. Even within such partnerships there will remain major questions around participation and the genuine sharing of vision and programmes. In Seattle for example the consultation process on the development of their 'Comprehensive Plan' (for a city of 550,000 people) cost $3.5 million over 3 years. Whilst I am not suggesting that such sums can realistically be made available here, participation, credibility and relevance go hand in hand and the issue has to be openly addressed.

Range of Outcomes. One way to help address this issue will be to devise a range of outcomes, some of which will be local and short term; others will be more structural and longer term. Again, this builds on the experience of others - for example, in Barcelona where great care was taken to try and address immediate priorities in working-class neighbourhoods across the city at the same time as decisions on larger scale infrastructure to facilitate the Olympic Games were taking place. But the outcomes must also vary in nature - from research projects that enable better understanding of the sub-region, to exemplary 'soft' projects which are about ways of doing things, to physical 'flagship' projects, to new institutions and partnerships.

The strategy itself. Finally in drafting the strategy, all those involved must remember that it has many purposes. It will for example seek to become an integral part of other people's strategies - such as the revised London Pride prospectus, the Association of London Government's work, of GOLs work, the work of the local TECs and of major partnerships. It will also provide the framework for accessing new and more resources from the major funding streams both in the UK and in Europe, but always emphasising it is primarily about what *we* will do here in the sub-region not just what *they* can do for us. It is worth emphasising here that there is also great scope and need to develop more successful bids with the voluntary sector that may be of a smaller scale and more innovative. There is a dangerous tendency for this kind of bid to be marginalised at present. It also needs to become the basis for clarifying and strengthening partnerships in the sub-region - that is the partnerships that will be necessary to implement the strategy.

Finally, it will be a document that sets out to change expectations about the sub-region's future. It will be about building confidence within and beyond the sub-region, linked to strategies for marketing and promotion.

In conclusion it is worth re-emphasising that the construction and ownership of such a strategy will not be easy - but it is better to see it as a challenge than a problem. Its successful implementation will no doubt be even more difficult. But there has never been a time to be more optimistic about the sub-region's potential. History will rightly judge us harshly if, collectively, we fail to turn that potential into reality. The ideas in this paper are to be worked up in association with a range of partners covering the whole of East London in the hope that it will be possible to prepare a jointly owned strategy for the sub-region of the kind argued for here.

The intention is to consult widely as the exercise gets under way, but if you have any comments on this initial paper, they would be very welcome. The contact address for comments is given at the front of the journal.

REFERENCES

Association of London Government, *Sustainable Urban Regeneration in London*, ALG, 1996.

Butler, T. and Rustin, M., *Rising in the East: The Regeneration of East London*, Lawrence and Wishart, London 1995.

Department of the Environment, *Thames Gateway Planning Framework*, 1995.

London East Training and Enterprise Council, *Corporate Plan*, LETEC, London 1996.

London Pride, *London Pride Action Programme*, London Pride, London 1996.

Perri 6, *Open Wide*, Demos, London 1996.

West London Leadership, *A Strategic Development Framework*, WWL, London 1996.

Wilkinson, H., *No Turning Back*, Demos, London 1996.

Wilkinson, H. and Mulgen, G., *Freedom's Children*, Demos, London 1995.

Thames Gateway London in the Millennium

Anna Whyatt

As we enter the twenty-first century, the forces shaping the global economy are changing the economic roles of nations and creating new demands on local and regional economies. The implications for regeneration in city regions are profound. Successful regions in the new millennium will be those able, through their leading edge sectors, to reach directly into the global economy. This article examines some of the key characteristics of successful regions for the future and looks at the development of the Thames Gateway London in the light of these.

THE THAMES GATEWAY LONDON is critical to London's success as a World City. It is the largest, most prominent development corridor in the capital with the greatest development and opportunity potential, employing 875,000 people - nearly one-third of all London jobs. It is also an economy in transition, poised between some of the worst economic decline in the capital at the same time as it offers potential for growth for the Millennium. The area has already begun to respond to these new challenges but is at a crucial moment in its history. The Thames Gateway London Partnership is a sub-regional alliance of twelve key local authorities, two Training and Enterprise Councils, English Partnerships and the London Docklands Development Corporation working together to bring about high quality sustainable regeneration throughout the Gateway. Successful regions in the new millennium will be those operating consistently through their leading sectors in today's global economy. What does this mean for the development of the Gateway and what are the implications for a new and ground-breaking alliance within the capital city?

As we enter the twenty first century, the forces shaping the global economy are changing the economic roles of nations and creating new demands on regional and local economies. Population growth, the internationalisation of markets around the three major trade blocks, the convergence of global consumer tastes, deregulation, and the advance of modern information technologies are all combining to transform the terms of competition and the way in which business operates. A pattern is emerging of international market dominance operated by a number of major players, also generating increasing opportunity for the Small and Medium-sized Enterprises (SME) sector. Technology transfer is leading to convergence between as well as inside previously disconnected sectors such as IT, telecommunications, and media, and creating new sectoral clusters. These in turn offer the potential of a leading edge position for particular locations in Europe. These changes in business operation are creating experimentation with corporate structures and an ability to gain access to labour at a global level. Employment patterns are changing, with increasingly segmented labour markets. There is demand for higher level skills recruited from an international as well as regional and national pools. Distance and life-time learning are set to revolutionise the delivery of training and education. (Business in the Community/Shell UK Ltd 1994, Hayes et al 1994).

These global determinants are shaping policy outcomes in historic and irreversible ways. A transformation is taking place comparable to the shifts of the first industrial revolution (Hayes et al 1994) which is outpacing the capability of institutional frameworks to respond. The ability of governments to understand and manage such changes will be a decisive factor for the future. The need for the UK to build such capability is urgent. There will be a need for public policy programmes which support development in a focused, functional context, supporting companies in achieving international excellence, and developing collaboration between firms and across sectors.

The implications for regeneration in city-regions are profound. One of the major implications of these international changes is the emergence of 'region states' (Ohmae 1995). Successful regions in the new millennium will be those 'with intelligence' able, through their leading edge sectors, to build agglomeration and competitiveness to reach directly into the global economy. Nation states will increasingly need these 'intelligent regions' to maximise job generation. A regional system which is able to achieve the maximum amount of responsiveness to market opportunity, blending elements of comparative advantage and growth pole strategies (Hutton 1995) will be critical for the future. Britain's regions are still too peripheral to European and global economic change and they are insufficiently competitive.

The key function for development agencies in this model is one of empowering, mobilising and networking. But these systems will need to be consciously developed. A favourable combination of local circumstances may not be enough to secure economic growth. Even where there is apparent market strength, this may be subject to rapid change as international market conditions alter. Cross-regional European research on successful regional intervention for job generation has emphasised a number of components of a regional policy framework. The most significant market advantages are likely to accrue to those regions able to offer and promote:

(1) Understanding based on intelligence and a developed research base of the strengths and sectoral opportunities for an area leading to a shared economic strategy which has a flexible method of implementation through an agency or with selected partners.

(2) Clear capacity to encourage convergence, with support for the transformation of key sectors through new forms of collaboration. The UK lacks sufficient clusters of horizontally and vertically linked firms to support the internationally competitive industries which underpin successful economies. The ability to achieve this depends as much on the development of new markets between the 'spaces' which convergence offers as continuing to support traditional industries. This can also mean support for future growth sectors both those which are known, for example in the environmental field - predicted job growth in Europe is 70 per cent between 1992 and 2000 - and those which are as yet uncharted, such as the futures technology field - the convergence for which is occurring between telecommunications, media, information technology and technology manufacturing which could result in the development of entirely new clusters of industrial activity.

(3) New approaches to developing business capability among SMEs by enabling more complex forms of collaboration between firms and across sectors. This will require a radical change in thinking about development to find a way through the current divide between 'a sustainable environment' and 'growth' - by the creation of a new 'clean technology' base.

(4) Building of the overall skill base to the appropriate international standard, both of management capability and skills clusters. This requires a shift of training and education systems to create an effective system of vocational training at higher order levels. The regional analysis of demand side requirements is identifying skills deficits as the major problem for employers. There is need for a major leap in skills capability to tackle increasing social polarisation. It is clear that the integration of individual commitment and learning with local

economic development will be key for successful local economies for the future. (Campbell 1994, National Advisory Committee on Education and Training Targets 1994). Regional economies which fail to take notice of this will run the risk of perpetuating a low skills trap where employers cease to look for skills capability in a particular geographical area because it is not being supplied.

(5) A flexible climate responding to prospective as well as current sectoral shifts. This requires at an industry level proactive support, a strong networking culture, and joint venture support services within the corporate sector. A properly resourced and networked business link system, functioning internationally with audio/visual facilities is an essential element of joint venture support services.

(6) Development of appropriate infrastructure, consisting of both 'hard' and 'soft' technology transfer systems, giving SME access to advanced technologies, expert advice and problem solving facilities, and improved frameworks for the creation and diffusion of technical know-how. Flexible, proactive and co-ordinated project handling and 'aftercare' support services for smaller companies, covering all aspects of the locational needs of firms, are needed.

(7) Regional labour market strategies which prevent economic re-structuring from falling disproportionately on the disadvantaged (Campbell 1994). These need to act to address mismatches of demand and supply, give improved access to employment, and reduce demand side barriers (Campbell 1995a).

(8) A capability to manage change to empower communities to embrace the challenges of the future, aligning individuals and companies with a collective vision. A high degree of political self-governance which allows policies in education, training, and technology to be tailored to the needs of the region (Tomaney 1995, Mawson 1995) is called for.

(9) Partnerships which are built on trust and good personal working relationships between individuals, institutions and associations with a deep commitment to the partnership. Effective management of local resources based on collaboration via a flexible method of implementation either through a semi-autonomous agency or through individual partners with the common strategy as a primary focus.

London, by virtue of its international profile, its historical base in key industries, its contribution to GDP and the size of its labour market, is at the forefront of these shifts in the UK. Their impact on the capital is reflected both in the way in which sectors and functions rather than spatial areas are now driving the London economy, and also in the way in which it is showing high levels of unemployment and long-term unemployment alongside internationally competitive functions such as business and financial services, tourism, and the arts (London TECs 1996). Failure to take account of international trends, for example in manufacturing, has resulted in a converse impact which flows back with negative consequences for the labour market and social polarisation. The overall result of this, for London as for other regions, is persistent skill mismatch resulting in a rise in long-term unemployment (Policy Studies Institute 1993), despite high levels of investment, environmental improvement and business activity. The spatial concentration of disadvantaged communities has led to polarised areas, with a division between job-rich and job-poor households and communities. Recent attempts to remedy these spatial imbalances have been based on the view that indigenous communities could generate compensating new employment.

In reality the dynamics of the economy are increasingly mobile, and focus on economic function rather than locality. It is increasingly clear that London's future as a World City, is now dependent upon its ability to develop its three key roles. These are:

- As a centre of decision-making, influence and prestige.
  Key functions: seat of governance; international banking and finance; commercial HQs.
- As a centre for production and distribution of goods.
  Key functions: gateway/logistics; manufacturing; producer services.
- As a centre for creativity and innovation.
  Key functions: technology futures; culture and arts; tourism.

The successful regeneration of local areas will increasingly depend upon the exploitation of broader opportunities within individual sectors, largely shaped by global forces. London must achieve this through the contribution of its sub-regions. These are:

- Central London: seat of governance, commercial command, banking and finance, tourism, arts and culture.
- West London: Gateway/logistics, technology futures, manufacturing, media and commercial command.
- South London: Retail/wholesale, manufacturing, business and financial services, logistics, tourism.
- North London: manufacturing, retail and logistics.

- Thames Gateway London: retailing, producer services, business and financial services, manufacturing, gateway/logistics, printing and tourism. (London TECs 1996)

Building the future Thames Gateway London

An Economy in Transition

The major changes which are shaping the global and London economy have resulted in radical change for Thames Gateway London. Extending from Hackney and the City fringe eastwards to Thurrock and southwards to Greenwich and Bexley, the Gateway has historically been a powerhouse of manufacturing and the main contributor to London's role as an international trading port. The last ten years has seen re-structuring within a settled nexus of older, traditional industries, alongside the emergence of new industrial and commercial activity. There have been major job losses in manufacturing. For the outer boroughs in the Gateway, the main change has been in the fast track development of support service industries in the 1970s, linked with the financial service industries, the growth of leisure and out-of town shopping, and the availability of large sites out of the central London area which have facilitated this development. At the southern end of the Gateway, in Lewisham, Bexley and Greenwich, change is taking place from a residential and dormitory role, to that of a key node for business services, manufacturing and tourism. For the inner areas of Tower Hamlets, Newham, Lewisham and Greenwich, based within 'the crescent of deprivation' in London's inner core, the change has been characterised primarily by a decline in traditional employment in the Docks, in manufacturing, and in printing. This development of the Thames Gateway London was not planned as such but has developed in response to both internal and external pressures. But these shifts are also happening within an international framework of change - in ownership, management process, and markets in both new and old sectors. This has meant that instead of a gradual transition with a 'bedding down' period of industrial re-settling, the area has borne year on year the impact of continuous re-structuring. As a result, the strengths of the area have become fragmented and disassociated, with geographic dispersal of the main industries. The sub-region remains poised midway between a circle of decline, on the one hand, and a circle of prosperity on the other.

Successful regions in the new millennium will be those operating consistently through their leading sectors in today's global economy. The

Thames Gateway London is critical to London's success as a World City. It is the largest, most prominent development corridor in the capital with the greatest development and opportunity potential. The area encompasses several key concentrations of dynamic commercial activity, interspersed with unrecognised areas of quality natural environment, with a strong manufacturing base and untapped potential in tourism and distribution and logistics. The Gateway currently employs 875,000 people; this is nearly one-third of all London jobs, which are very locally based - 58 per cent of the residents work in their local area. The Gateway now has the opportunity to become an effective and growing sub-region with private-public sector regeneration partnerships able to reach directly into the global economy.

To achieve this level of change for the sub-region will not be easy. It is clear that Thames Gateway London is currently under-performing and that it must develop its emergent functions as rapidly as possible whilst consolidating its current asset base. The capability of its resident workforce falls far short of that of the other sub-regions of the capital. The need for quality skills, at an internationally competitive level, has led to a serious mismatch between labour market opportunities and the human resources available. There is therefore urgent need to promote a major upgrading of skills throughout the area. Without collaborative effort around an agenda for development of the key functions, the sub-region is likely to shift into decline. The area has already begun to respond to these new challenges but is at a crucial moment in its history. Its development strategy needs to change direction to enable it to realise its sub-regional potential and to make its full contribution to the London of the twenty-first century. The Thames Gateway London Partnership is a sub-regional alliance of twelve key local authorities, two Training and Enterprise Councils, English Partnerships and the London Docklands Development Corporation working together with the private sector and community to bring about high quality sustainable regeneration of the whole of Thames Gateway London. The Partnership is committed to the importance of improving the competitiveness of business and the workforce in its area. But the area is struggling with fragmentation, lack of overall leadership and too few initiatives that will make the difference at a national and international level of competitiveness. A key plank in the development of the sub-region is the drawing together of an economic strategy to provide a framework designed to structure the development of the area over the next decade. In taking the strategy forward partner organisations will be acting to combine their considerable individual assets and capabilities to maximise and add value across the sub-region.

Building up key economic roles

Sector development is extremely weak in this country compared with that which takes place elsewhere in Europe - for example in Baden Wurttenberg, Nord Pas de Calais, Emilia Romagna, Valencia, and Catalonia, or in the clustering of the German Mittelstand companies where strong regional sectoralism is supported by an infrastructure of technical expertise, including technology transfer, operated and accessed on a collective basis. Strong emphasis is placed in these regions on maintaining a competitive level of performance in order to capture and retain niches in the world market. Some good UK examples of 'regional sectoralism' are the South Coast Metropole (Southampton, Portsmouth, Poole and Bournemouth) which focuses on new marine technology products, the Hertfordshire sub-region (pharmaceutical growth through partnership between local universities and firms, complemented by training strategies), and the Northern Development Company (Black and Decker, Electrolux, Thorne Lighting Co and Nissan) developing supply chains and appropriate forms of training. Thames Gateway London needs comparable forms of sectoral partnership.

- *A centre of excellence for manufacturing, research and development, environmental manufacturing, computing and electronics and a key focus for technology futures.*

This needs to be backed by research and development, building on the current key industrial clusters, and supporting the emergence of new manufacturing businesses. The sector still offers the second largest concentration of manufacturing output and employment in the capital with positive performance compared to London as a whole. It has London's largest concentration of manufacturing firms (1 in 5 of London manufacturing jobs) and embraces all sub-sectors of manufacturing. It is concentrated at Barking and Dagenham, Havering, Tower Hamlets, Redbridge and Belvedere. Already an internationally recognised centre for research into manufacturing, the Gateway is beginning to develop in the technology futures area with a major initiative for a Technology College at the Royal Docks, and activity in South London which provides access for the companies of the future. The relocation of the publishing and printing industry into Docklands has developed the industry as a major focus for growth with evidence of renewed activity and confidence at key regeneration sites. 80 per cent of the 4.5 million square feet within Canary Wharf Phase 1 is now occupied.

- *An international tourism, cultural industries and heritage venue*

    The Gateway is set to become London's second international tourism venue at the Pool of London, Spitalfields and Liverpool Street, the Royal Docks, and the Greenwich Peninsula, via the Millennium Exhibition. There is the potential to create innovative new tourist centres, for example at the Royal Docks. These existing flagships are backed by a supporting infrastructure of many museums and galleries, at Walthamstow, Stoke Newington, Bethnal Green and Tower Hamlets. There is some fine open space at Havering, Epping Forest and Thurrock. There is a major regional retailing venue at Lakeside. Liverpool Street, Stratford, Stansted and London City Airport provide strong transport linkages into Europe, the City and West End, with transport enhancements which will have cost £4.5bn. The sub-region offers proximity to central London, a strong asset base in heritage and tourism attractions, and many large ex-industrial sites for development. The Gateway should be able to provide many of the new hotel complexes which London now needs.

- *A major distribution, logistics and passenger transport node.*

    Through the opportunities created by new routeways to Europe, both south and north of the Thames, there is opportunity to create a satellite node for business and financial services.

- *An internationally known centre of academic excellence linked to industrial excellence through new centres of innovation.*

    There are eleven colleges and three universities - the Universities of East London, Greenwich and London University.

- *A satellite node for business and financial services*

    This needs to be created by working with the City of London to access the overspill of the industry from the City and West End, but also offering facilities at the southern end of the Gateway and local firms to capture an international niche in the market.

- *Developing the new markets between the 'spaces' which convergence offers with a clear capacity to encourage and create convergence by enabling much more complex forms of collaboration and SME growth between firms and across sectors.*

    The capacity to achieve regional regeneration depends as much on development of new markets between the 'spaces' which convergence offers as on continuing to support traditional industries. It requires an ability to facilitate interdependent networks of SMEs able to internationalise, to sub-contract to one another, and to benefit from the tendency for multinationals to decentralise into lower federations of operating units and associated sub-contractors. In many of the successful European regions, firms have access to funding and banks linked to their industrial sector. The purpose of this is two-fold - to create an environment where small and medium-sized firms can o perate as partners for multinationals and to promote linkages between large firms and SMEs, avoiding the 'branch plant syndrome'. The potential for SME development has been identified by all international futures predictions including the OECD (OECD 1994). Between-sector opportunities are as important as those occurring inside sectors. There is also need to widen the concept of enterprise, covering self-employment, co-operatives, and non-profit organisations, fostering the culture of entrepreneurship in wider segments of the population. There is need to develop support structures which recognise that the founders of modern small enterprise embrace people of all ages, genders and races as opposed to the stereotypical white male. There need to be incentives and support which ease the transition of small scale innovative enterprises into the future mainstream.

There is a synergy between several of the key economic functions of the Gateway. The area has many clusters of mutually-supportive independent small firms with a strong potential for further growth and cross-sector activity. A more co-ordinated and focused approach will be needed to develop the critical mass required amongst SMEs in particular sectors. However, there are a number of key industrial clusters, in business and financial services, and in print and publishing, which remain relatively unexploited. Other areas in which the Gateway is strong are health, environmental and personal services, and education. The recent European Commission investigation into 'Local development and Employment Initiatives' identified 17 fields having the potential for this type of employment creation (Marks 1994). It is crucial to ensure that these areas in turn assist convergence and the strengthening of the sectoral base in a region, through support for multiple forms of small company development and by linking into private sector market development, for example in associated manufacturing. In distance and modular learning, for example, there are clear applications in the technology futures area and in the environmental field, with products and services ranging from combined heat and power plants to electric motor vehicles. The sub-region is also strong in SME clustering. Of the total number of businesses, the majority are small. Seventy-five per cent of business have up to 10 employees, 10 per cent are medium-sized, only one per cent are large, with over 200 employees. The strongest job-creation potential in the Gateway area has been identified as existing within the small firm size-band. The Gateway has an overall business performance level in all sectors (except for transport and retail) which supersedes that of London as a whole. Business growth in the area was fifty two per cent between 1980 and 1982 compared to a regional figure of forty four per cent and by eight per cent between 1989 and 1991 compared to sic per cent for London.

The Thames Gateway has already begun to respond to the new challenges. The potential for new clusters of economic activity to emerge within key economic functions, and the unexploited potential in each area of linkage present huge opportunities for future growth. This applies to those sectors which are being redefined by convergence and are at the cutting edge of niche-market development as well as those within 'conventional' sectoral clusters. But they are still too embryonic and weak in market terms to survive without a public policy framework which sustains their growth, whilst at the same time ensuring that the benefits which flow from growth are accessible to residents. A strongly integrated policy approach for the development of each function, and intelligence and support for the transformation of key sectors, will be needed. This will involve agreement on the priorities for action in the area, support for those projects which will deliver maximum benefit to the sub-region, and a full strategy for inward investment targeted on the six economic priorities.

One of the areas on which these issues will impact most strongly is business support. World class business needs world class business support (Grayson 1994). There is no consistent support system operating in the English regions comparable to those within the leading European regions. Business leaders have become increasingly concerned about the weakness of the business support system, including organisation for inward investment, lobbying for and management of European funding, and regional strategic planning (Business in the Community/Shell Ltd 1994).

A further key area of impact derives from the potential resource which derives from ethnic diversity. There needs to be a cultural change which leads to the development of economic initiative in all sections of the population. Cultural diversity and pluralism should be seen as a positive resource in developing competitive culture, rather than as a barrier to success, as it is often viewed in the UK. The sub-region, especially Newham and Tower Hamlets, has the largest cultural diversity of any region in Europe, with potential for establishing major links with the Pacific Basin and Asia as springboards for future market development. For example, over one million people visit the Spitalfields mosque each year. The sub-region needs to be one where ethnic diversity is valued. Partnerships need to be established to support black and Asian business development in the area.

Development of appropriate infrastructure

Supporting key roles and functions - strengthening key development areas and the transportation infrastructure

One of the major levers for delivering economic change in the sub-region will be the development of the key geographic nodes - that is, geographic centres of existing and potential growth, which have the required 'critical mass' in emerging functions and sectors. These comprise five main groups which are summarised in the table below:

GROUP	PRIMARY NODE	SECONDARY NODE
International and national tourism/heritage venues	Isle of Dogs, Canary Wharf/ Royal Docks, Eastern Fringe of the City including Spitalfields and the Goods Yard/ Trueman's Brewery Sites, Tower Hill, Pool of London, St. Katherine's Dock, Greenwich and Woolwich	Waltham Forest and the entrance to the Lee valley/ Epping Forest, Aldgate and Bow, Deptford Creekside, Ebbsfleet Valley
Established manufacturing/ industrial districts currently undergoing change	Thameside corridor from Rainham through Barking and Dagenham to Beckton/ Romford/Ilford corridor/Tower Hamlets, Bexley, Belvedere / Ebbsfleet	Eastern Fringe of the City, including Spitalfields, Aldgate and Bow, Waltham Forest, Lee Valley Science Park
Major passenger transport intersections	Stratford and the railands, Thurrock/Port of Tilbury	Deptford Creekside
Town centres and related office developments	Ilford and Romford /Lewisham Town Centre/Bexleyheath	
Primary venues for business and technology futures	Isle of Dogs, Canary Wharf/ Royal Docks, Lee Valley Science Park	

The globalisation currently driving London's key sectors is reflected in a corresponding demand for international quality transport. A transport infrastructure which facilitates business growth emerges as the priority element on which success in all sectors depends. All the proposed and projected transport schemes are essential to development in the Thames Gateway London. Without them the prospects of manufacturing, tourism and logistics in particular will be seriously inhibited. Transport infrastructure is currently the element being most strongly developed in the Gateway, but isolated from the development of other sectors, and with little business rationale. To secure success, transport support must be directed to the requirements of the key economic sectors. Transport initiatives in Thames Gateway London need to be re-oriented to obtain the maximum economic benefit, particularly at the key nodes. Access to international airport connections at Heathrow, Gatwick and City Airport and to European rail connections at Waterloo and Stratford are particularly vital for the development of business and financial services, and tourism. Stronger links with global corporate networks can be based on London City Airport (now making progress), on access to Stansted Airport, and on the international national rail passenger transport station at Stratford. There is need to build linkages between the different networks of rail, tube and air transport. There is also need for the enhanced use of the River Thames for leisure, passenger use, and freight. This is as critical for central London as it is for the Gateway.

There are insufficient intra-region transport connections both in public transport and road to facilitate ease of access between key centres in inner and outer parts of the sub-region. This is especially true for tourism, but also impacts upon academic services, logistics, and technology futures. There is similarly a lack of intra-region road networks to give good access to key outside locations such as airports. Road access into key nodes and centres is poor, especially at Greenwich/Woolwich, Walthamstow, and Deptford Creekside. There needs to be an examination of the public transport system to consider improvements to intra-regional travel, including the possible provision of a light rail transit system.

Support from London-wide lobbies and project-specific borough campaigns have resulted in major changes in schemes such as the Jubilee Line and East London Line (Northern) extensions, and the Docklands Light Rail extension. However, there remain a number of major schemes which are not yet committed, which are vital to the development of the sub-region. A strategic lobby programme in relation to transport needs to put into operation by the Thames Gateway Partnership.

Developing a world class workforce

The development of key economic sectors, and of employment, are the keys to the future. Growth must be accompanied by the eradication of economic exclusion, and by the ability for cultural diversity to make a significant contribution to economic success.

Obviously, a highly trained and skilled workforce is the key to economic success. Every economic initiative must be backed by a strong education and training framework. There are dramatic implications for the labour force of European integration, globalisation, technological convergence and industrial restructuring, and of changes in employment patterns and working arrangements. At the individual level there is a continuing trend towards work in part-time, portfolio, self-employed or short-contract arrangements. The portfolio/jobs cluster segments of the labour market - currently the second thirty per cent of Hutton's 30-30-40 society (Hutton 1995), is growing. Even for those who remain within a conventional pattern of full-time work, continuous updating of skills will be required (CBI 1994). Increasing numbers of individuals will need voluntarily to 'own' marketable skill-clusters, whether at any one time they are in or out of work. The combination of individual demand and higher geographical mobility means that firms are able to recruit and access labour internationally.

A number of 'decision-spaces' now exist in London in which purchasers of labour seek to engage with sellers of labour. This results in a hierarchy of overlapping and nested labour markets - at the international, national, regional, sub-regional and local level. The nature of operation of this hierarchy of labour markets is such that the potential for exclusion of those without higher level skills is now great.

Thames Gateway London currently provides approximately 875,000 jobs. The resident workforce is projected to grow by 22,000 by 2001. Older workers will increase by 22 per cent and the proportion of women workers by 2 per cent to 46 per cent within this period. An increase of 8 per cent is projected in part-time employment. Most Gateway residents are heavily dependent upon public transport. Approximately 58 per cent of the residents work in their local area. Only Barking and Dagenham and Tower Hamlets were net importers of labour between 1981 and 1991. Twenty-nine per cent of jobs in the Gateway are taken by inward commuters, mainly from Essex. Structural changes are impacting on Gateway residents more severely than on other sub-regions of the capital. This is reflected in the unemployment levels in the Gateway and in the way in which unemployment has risen consistently, within the same areas between 1991 and 1994. The combination of de-industrialisation in specific locations, and downsizing in public sector organisations which have traditionally offered semi-skilled to unskilled jobs, with the spatial distribution of low-cost housing has created a spiral of unemployment in the 'crescent' from the City and Hackney through inner East London and cross-river to Lewisham, Southwark, and Lambeth. The situation in the outer Gateway boroughs is very different, with general levels of unemployment below national and London averages, but with pockets of significant unemployment in some areas.

We can summarise the key elements of change in Thames Gateway London's labour market. These are:

- A move to the dominance of services and distribution - more than 50 per cent of all jobs in the Gateway area.
- Relatively high manufacturing employment notwithstanding losses in this sector. Employment is increasingly in pharmaceutical, electrical and automotive engineering, electronics, printing, publishing, utilities and transport and communications. 16-18 per cent of all jobs.
- Re-structuring of the labour market - resulting in increased self-employment, contract and temporary work - is leading to

  (i) demand for increased capability of individuals to respond to new patterns of working, to the need for transferable skills, and to the rapid development of skills clusters;

  (ii) a blurring of divisions between home and work;

  (iii) a low level of job vacancies - in 1995 74 per cent of establishments in London East reported no current vacancies;
- An increasing need for individual mobility to find jobs - 37 per cent of residents work outside the sub-region, mainly in the City and inner London.
- A significantly young age profile. Newham has the highest proportion of households with children under 5 years of age (18 per cent) in the UK but Tower Hamlets and Barking and Dagenham also have young populations.
- High overall unemployment. In 1995, there were approximately 105,000 unemployed in the Gateway area. There were exceptionally high levels of unemployment in specific local areas across the Gateway. In some wards of Newham and Tower Hamlets this reached 32 per cent, and within specific groups (e.g. men in the 25-34 age group). There is disproportionately high unemployment (23 per cent) in ethnic

minority communities and an increasing proportion of long-term unemployed (62 per cent of all unemployed in 1995).

- Low levels of attainment and aspiration amongst young people. GCSE attainment in the area is lower than the UK average, but there has also been more rapid improvement in the last three years (Watson 1996). There is a low full-time staying-on rate among pupils at 16 - young people are not staying on long enough to obtain NVQ Level 3 qualifications. GCE 'A' level pass rates were far below the UK average. Examination results in the Thames Gateway London outer boroughs are worse than in other parts of outer London (Watson 1996).

- High levels of deprivation. The Gateway encompasses the poorest urban areas in the UK and Northern Europe. Newham ranks first, Tower Hamlets seventh, Lewisham eleventh, and Greenwich fourteenth in deprivation scores for local authorities in the UK (LRC 1995, HMSO 1995).

These trends highlight the following critical issues for the sub-region:

- An overriding problem of skill mismatch and skills deficit. Over the next five years there will be a rise in the number of technical, professional, managerial posts comprising 37 per cent of total employment in the area with a significant increase in demand for NVQ level 3 and above (SOLOTEC/LETEC Economic Assessments 1996). Overall, the skill levels of residents in the Gateway are significantly lower than in London as a whole. Local residents are unable to access high skill and craft related jobs in the areas of health and professions, managerial, personal and engineering services, administration and associate professional.

- A predominance of employment in lower level skills when demand will be for higher skills and for the management of smaller companies, with the expected increase in SME activity. A much lower percentage (30 per cent) are employed in higher grade skill areas, than in London as a whole (40 per cent).

- Overall employment prospects are strongest for higher level skills but the TGL has a much lower levels of skill capability than in other sub-regions of the capital. At present only one in ten are qualified to NVQ level 4 in London East and 41 per cent to NVQ level 3 in the SOLOTEC area (compared with 44.6 per cent London-wide). There is low GCSE and 'A'-level attainment compared to the national average. The degree to which existing skills are transferable is in doubt. A considerable programme of training for local people related to future job opportunities needs to be established before local people will be able to access jobs in the London growth sectors.

- Growth of existing businesses will not be sufficient to ensure full employment for the local population. The complexity of movement within the London labour market and the Rest of the South East (ROSE) means that a much more sophisticated, London-wide strategy is required to ensure that jobs are accessible by those in local communities in need of work. The integration of individual commitment and learning into local economic development in mutually reinforcing ways will be key for successful local economies for the future (Campbell 1995b). Increased learning and enhanced skills not only meet the demands of changing labour markets, but also generate new demand for skills, once these are seen to be available. Regional economies which fail to take notice of this will run the risk of perpetuating a low skills trap where employers cease to look for skills capability in a particular geographical area. Solving this problem will require re-alignment of delivery systems to deliver necessary skill capabilities, including systems for self-directed learning and distance learning. There is also need for incentives to improve skills, both for employers and individuals - for example by 'tax-breaks'. A constantly re-skilling and flexible workforce backed by an electronic infrastructure will in future be the only true source of competitive advantage.

The Thames Gateway London Partnership aims to create a sub-region known in Europe for its innovative skills. Its strategy must encompass several strands:

1. Consistent monitoring of the human resource requirements that arise from sectoral opportunities in the Thames Gateway London. This requires the development of a strategic audit and evaluation system in each of the key functions to anticipate skills demand and to identify the skills standards required - in manufacturing sub-sectors, cultural industries, tourism-associated industries logistics, academic and business and financial services via the sector training networks.

2. The establishment of focused spheres of excellence in training in the key sectors for the Gateway. These may take the form of physical centres, or of developed expertise located in specific organisations. Examples of such centres are the proposed technology college in the Royals for technology futures and associated industries; Greenwich University, for the arts, tourism, and associated industries.

3. The provision of skills to match demand as part of a matrix of attractions to investors. And, as part of a strategy for retention of investment, a comprehensive labour market strategy to which all partners subscribe. A considerable programme of training for local people related to future job opportunities will need to be established before local people will be able to access jobs in London's growth sectors. There should be a local recruitment campaign to introduce employers to the skills available within the sub-region.

4. Support for the emergence of the skills capabilities which will be needed for the emerging SME sector. Promote greater training access within SMEs on a consortium basis, within sectors and at management level.

5. The empowerment of firms, institutions, individuals and communities to manage and access the opportunities offered by change. This will mean the identification and provision of core skills clusters for professional, managerial and technical occupations, skills training and strategic management skills for managing changes within the technology transfer nexus. This will mean:
    - An increase in higher quality vocational education with links to other institutions for education in later life;
    - The special targeting of young people to offer vocational courses alongside GCSEs during the final two years of secondary schooling;
    - A campaign to encourage a higher level of staying-on rates at school and college.

6. Changes in process and provision of the delivery of education and training to respond to structural changes in employment. Specifically:
    - review current programmes in terms of scale, appropriateness and quality;
    - review access and information systems and significant upgrading;
    - increase the use of more flexible training delivery from opening hours to the use of multi-media technology;
    - develop modern apprenticeships as a high quality, high qualification programme;
    - monitor the provision and evaluate the impact of new training products with regard to appropriateness and the raising of quality standards;
    - ensure IT is established as a core skill.

- To undertake this the Thames Gateway Partnership Board has agreed in principle to establish a Thames Gateway London 21st Century Skills Commission to co-ordinate and drive forward a programme to promote life-time learning and skills development at all levels in the Thames Gateway. Its aim is to achieve a fundamental change in attitudes towards training and skills amongst individuals and businesses.

From the cycle of decline to the circle of prosperity

Regional labour market strategies are required to relieve the potential for the 'locking out' of specific groups from the labour market, and to try to prevent the costs of economic re-structuring from falling disproportionately on the already disadvantaged, with a further widening of income, social and geographical inequalities (Campbell 1995b). There is widespread agreement on this. People without skills are five times more likely to become unemployed than those with higher education level qualifications (Campbell 1995b). The regional analysis of demand side requirements is identifying skills deficits, not skill shortages, as the major problem for employers. There is also evidence from local skills audits that the long-term unemployed include many with higher order skills. It follows that enhancement of the portfolio of skills of the long-term unemployed, rather than their complete retraining, should be an aim. For this to happen there would need to be better access systems, to enable the long-term unemployed to participate in new sector development through a mix of measures including personal support, benefit flexibility, placement and wage subsidies. The emphasis of support, including training and education, should be re-directed towards the long-term unemployed. There needs to be more integration of the long-term unemployed in mainstream activity.

There are a number of issues in relation to the unemployed in the Gateway which need further investigation. These include:

- a review of the nature of unemployment amongst Gateway residents and development of more innovative, targeted methods to reduce it;
- the development of an outward mobility strategy;
- greatly improved access and guidance systems to provide bridges to work. Improve access to information to enable business and individuals to capitalise on new working arrangements;
- establishment of a monitoring and assessment system to oversee the

effectiveness of access to information and guidance by adults and young people;
- an increase in modular and self-directed life-time learning linked to opportunity to obtain formal qualifications. The establishment of skills audits in local areas to identify those who could access jobs;
- an appropriate information and analysis system in relation to prospective skills requirements, current provision and unemployment and mobility. A system is required which collates and assesses information via a centralised database, and allows sharing and exchange of information between institutions;
- an investigation of the scale and nature of the apparent literacy and numeracy gap in the Gateway, and to develop proposals to meet the gap appropriately;
- the expansion of customised training provision, since this has repeatedly shown above-average success rates at competitive costs;
- a campaign to improve the attainment levels of young people through enhanced pre-school provision, attainment in core educational skills, and higher staying on rates for 16-year olds;
- Develop a strategic plan for delivery of childcare provision at the scale required.

Each of these strands needs to identify priority short-term programmes, with a dedicated segment targeted at ethnic minority communities where rates of unemployment are significantly above average, by any measure.

Making connections

Developing a capability to manage change

The achievement of the potential of individuals, of companies, and of the region is of course a widely-held aspiration, together with a commitment to inclusion and social integration. These are both moral issues, and at the same time are preconditions of business competitiveness. Opportunities lie in convergence and synergy between the needs of the individual and the needs of the market. Successful regions for the future will be those able to achieve the maximum amount of responsiveness to market opportunity whilst themselves creating new markets. Integration between the mainstream economy and the areas of deprivation and disadvantage are required, rather than these two economies being left to run, to their mutual disadvantage, on separate tracks.

Various partnerships are struggling to achieve that integration, but this process needs a much larger change of culture. The difficulty is that there are few tested models of sub-regional development. We find ourselves with twenty-first century thinking and nineteenth century delivery mechanisms. For example, the model of company assistance in the inner areas is still primarily an extension of the nineteenth century philanthropic model of 'doing good' despite the interventions of Business in the Community, London First, the Association of London Government, LPAC and others to put forward the business case for promoting economic activity in such areas. Yet within the next decade the same clusters of skills which will be required of individuals will be needed for companies and regions - capacity to manage change, empowering individuals and organisations, managing self and others, utilising skills, and to achieving common purpose, building teams and partnerships. Successful companies achieve alignment between the aspirations of individual, team and company (Covey 1994). Quantum leap change in inner area economies can only come about through similar alignments. There is a need to move out of the command and control paradigm and into the networking-team working paradigm. This is what is happening in the best companies and international institutions. There is already a great deal of partnership activity in the Thames Gateway London:

- collaboration between boroughs;
- private/public sector partnerships including the London Docklands Development Corporation;
- co-operation between TECs, boroughs and the private sector HE/FE/ borough/TEC joint working;
- establishment of the Thames Gateway London Partnership.

However these activities are characterised by their lack of overall co-ordination. There is a dominance of single projects which fail to build the necessary critical mass in sectors. Too much activity is small-scale, and it falls short of penetrating international markets. In general within the partnership there is a preponderance of meetings which fail to generate the required outputs. This leads to despondency and frustration. Scarce human resources are being stretched too thinly. There is a need to re-group and adopt a different method of operation.

The Thames Gateway London Partnership is gaining strength as an alliance. It has prepared a draft Economic Strategy on which it intends to consult by the Spring of 1997. Bringing the techniques of leading edge companies to developing the right kind of culture and context for the o peration of partnership - building ownership, trust and mutuality may enable many simultaneous changes to take place. For example, developing a learning culture (Hayes and Fonda 1996), stimulating the development of individual capabilities, and creating social inclusion across institutions and communities. This approach might assist the Thames Gateway Partnership to become an unstoppable force for economic change, mirroring the visionary strategies of other urban regions in Europe in setting direction, concentrating effort, providing consistency and ensuring the flexibility needed for the new Millennium.

The author would like to acknowledge the financial support of the Partnership and the considerable input and practical advice from member individuals and organisations.

REFERENCES

Business in the Community/Shell UK Ltd, *Work in Society*, BITC, London.

Campbell, M. A., 'Strategic approach to the local labour market' in M. Campbell and K. Duffy, *Local Labour Markets, Problems and Policies*, Longman, Harlow 1994.

Campbell, M. (1995a) 'Society without work? key issues and local responses', Paper prepared for LEDA workshop, July 1995.

Campbell, M. (1995b) 'Learning pays: individual commitment, learning and economic development', Leeds Metropolitan University, Leeds 1995.

Confederation of British Industry, *Individuals and Learning*, Employment Department/CBI Conference report, 1994.

Covey, S., *The Seven Habits of Highly Effective People*, Simon and Schuster, London 1994.

Grayson, D., 'Work in society', *Royal Society of Arts Journal*, February 1994, pp62-80.

Hayes C., N. Fonda & J. Hillman, *Learning in the New Millennium*, National Commission on Education, London 1994.

Hayes C, N. Fonda, *The University for Industry and Organisational Learning*, Confidential Working Pa per, 1996.

HMSO, *London Facts and Figures*, HMSO, London 1995.

Hutton, W., *The State We're In*, Vantage, London 1995.

London East TEC, *London East Economic Assessment*, University of East London/LETEC, London 1996.

London East TEC, *Corporate Plan*, 1996.

London Research Centre, *London Statistics*, 1995.

London TECs, Government Office for London and London First, *An Economic Profile of London*, South Bank University in association with GHK Ltd, London 1996.

Marks, S., *Europe's local challenge*, Paper presented to 1994 CLES Conference, 1994.

Mawson, J., 'The changing roles of the regions in local and central relations in Britain', Paper presented to the Joseph Rowntree Foundation, Birmingham 1995.

Organization for Economic Co-operation and Development, *Economic Surveys United Kingdom*, OECD, Paris 1994.

Ohmae, K., *Death of the Nation State*, Heinemann, London 1995.

South London TEC, *Economic Assessment*, University of East London in association with GHK Economics and Management, London 1996.

Tomaney, J., 'Regional government: possibilities and limits', Centre for Urban and Regional Studies, University of Newcastle Working paper, 1995.

Watson, J., An Education Audit of the Thames Gateway, Unpublished paper, University of Greenwich, 1996.

Building a Mosque in Stepney

Ethnic Minorities and the Planning System

Robert Home

Ethnic minorities may find themselves disadvantaged in their dealings with the system of land use planning, which mediates inter-group conflicts, and may protect the cultural codes and preferences of the dominant social group. The search by such minorities for places of worship involves them in a negotiation with the planning system, in an often disputed claim to territory and identity. This article examines the response of the planning system to such demands, with case studies of planning policy in Newham and a mosque in Stepney.

EAST LONDON is part of a capital city full of cultural diversity, in which nearly two hundred languages are spoken apart from English. A quarter of the resident population of inner London are non-white, compared with 5.5 per cent of the total British population (according to the 1991 census, the first to ask a specific question about ethnicity).

East London, because of its proximity to the docks, has been a reception area for refugees and economic migrants over centuries. While there were no regulations specifying areas of ethnic residence (unlike the ghettos of some European cities or the racial zoning of South Africa), small ethnic enclaves tended to become self-perpetuating through the processes of chain migration, drawing immigrants to areas where their compatriots had preceded them. On the City fringes Spitalfields had a long association with Flemish, Dutch and Walloon weavers, and absorbed Huguenot silk-weaving refugees in the late seventeenth century. Whitechapel was a centre for non-Jewish Germans in the late eighteenth century, then for East European Jews in the late nineteenth, and the Sephardic cemetery on the Mile End Road is the oldest surviving Jewish cemetery in the country, having been founded in 1657 (Merriman 1993).

The twentieth century, especially during its second half, has seen London's immigrants from Europe outnumbered by those from Africa, Asia and the Caribbean, as a result of the decline of the British empire (Rex 1973, Fryer 1984). In the words of Professor Stuart Hall, 'As they hauled down the flag, we got on the banana boat and sailed right into London ... to the centre of the hub of the world' (quoted in Jacobs 1996: 71). Docklands was associated with sailors from all over the world, and some of these communities have survived the extinction of the docks, with the continuing Chinese presence in Limehouse and the Somali community of Tower Hamlets. Members of the Commonwealth were free to enter Britain until legal controls over immigration were introduced in 1962. After World War Two the Bangladeshis, whose ancestors first arrived as lascar sailors, came to replace the Jews in the textile industry. Centuries of overseas colonial activity by Britain have created the cultural diversity of London. As the new communities say, 'We're here because you were there'.

The academic community has, however, only lately begun to address the issues raised by such cultural diversity, through research into race and ethnicity among local communities (Cohen 1995). The Museum of London and the Commission for Racial Equality have each developed an exhibition and book on the history of this diversity (Merriman 1993, CRE 1996). New academic discourses in cultural geography and postcolonialism are now exploring the consequences of conflicting 'territories of meaning' between different communities (Jackson 1989, Jacobs 1996). The University of East London's New Ethnicities Unit has examined issues of race and ethnicity both locally and globally (e.g. Cooper and Tarek Qureishi 1993). Its study of the Isle of Dogs, where the old and new East End meet head on, examines the role of discourses of race, class and ethnicity in linking the construction of identity to narratives of place, shaping perceptions of education, housing and the local state (Cohen, Tarek Qureishi and Toon 1993). Racism has a long history in East London (Husbands 1983), and politically local government is still disproportionately dominated by the white community. The situation was not helped by the abolition of the Greater London Council in 1986, which removed an elected strategic body which was trying to address issues of race inequality.

New approaches to cultural geography are exploring the way in which the urban landscape and built environment becomes a contested object of negotiation between the rival social groups who inhabit it. Cultural diversity finds itself reflected in struggles and negotiations over urban space. The social production of space, in both material and ideological terms, may deny ethnic minorities advantage and access, and, indeed, the very term ethnic minority tends to place them in a subordinate, alien and disadvantaged position. Furthermore, global shifts in the patterns of production and consumption can affect such diverse communities at a local level. An example would be the geographical proximity of high-value City offices and the grim living conditions of the Bangladeshi residents of Spitalfields, with the redevelopment of Spitalfields a contest between alternative views of the urban built environment (Rhodes and Nabi 1992).

In day-to-day living the physical forms of the urban landscape are adapted to the new communities' cultural patterns and codes, both within buildings and in land use patterns. Ethnic minority household sizes may be greater than the national average of slightly over two persons, creating different demands and pressure upon living space. Many cultures separate strangers from residents, and many include the sacred in the home through shrines, special places for prayer, ritual washing and religious gatherings (NFHA 1993). Muslim and Orthodox Jewish households need separate cooking arrangements for men and women, while contact with unclean animals, which may include dogs and cats, in some cultures necessitate ritual purification afterwards. Ethnic minorities may use residential property for business more than the general population. Small shops may assume a greater importance in ethnic minority community life, and shops, clubs and restaurants may expect to follow specialized dietary codes (e.g. slaughtering livestock in the halal style). There may be special ethnic requirements in shop front design, advertisements and lettering styles. Planning and conservation area controls may even seek to enhance the character of a ethnic minority area in order to promote tourism (e.g. the Chinatown area of Soho).

With such differing cultural values playing upon the built environment, the system of land use regulation assumes a particular importance in mediating inter-group conflicts, and often has functioned to protect the cultural codes and preferences of the dominant social group ('When in Rome, do as the Romans do'). As this article will explore, the search by ethnic minorities for places of worship involves them in a negotiation with the dominant population, mediated through the planning system, in an often disputed claim to territory and identity.

Race and the planning system

Despite the rapid growth of immigration into Britain after the end of World War Two, the planning system has been slow to acknowledge any need for policies to address the spatially concentrated needs of black and ethnic minorities. Thomas (1995) found an 'imperviousness of both political and professional decision-making in planning to the influence of black and ethnic minorities':

> The initial widespread reaction is that the scrupulous bureaucratic formality which planners have perfected over decades is a guarantee that there will be no racial discrimination exercised within the planning system. The system, being depersonalized, is 'colour blind'; and any attemnpt to modify that principle will threaten the integrity of the planning system itself and create practical difficulties in the working lives of planners. (Thomas 1995: 135)

Planners have shown a reluctance to address social welfare issues, so that bureaucracies committed to formal equality could unwittingly consolidate inequalities. The very term given to the British land use regulatory system - 'town and country planning' - itself implies the preservation of a geographical divide which has tended to discriminate against ethnic minorities. Maintaining a separation of town and country, through policies of urban containment and the protection of rural areas from development, has served to maintain constructions of rurality and English national identity which have excluded the non-white population. Rural areas remain ones in which black people feel, and are often made to feel, uncomfortable and unwelcome. The long-running planning dispute over the Hindu temple at Letchmore Heath, Hertfordshire, donated by the Beatle George Harrison to the Society of Krishna Consciousness, reflects indigenous sensitivities about protecting the 'Englishness' of the Hertfordshire Green Belt. Urban policy for the inner city, by contrast, has tended to become associated with issues of race. There was no explicit spatial policy in relation to immigration (i.e. defining where they should settle), although the Cullingworth Report (1969) recommended the dispersal of 'coloured immigrants' through housing allocation policies, spreading them out so that they would be submerged within the general population, even at the price of a loss of necessary support and identity from their own communities.

The emergence of the 'inner city problem', and particularly the Brixton and Toxteth disturbances of 1981, raised the profile of black and ethnic issues in a planning profession with a deep-rooted technocratic orientation. Section 71 of the Race Relations Act 1976 already required local authorities to ensure that their various functions were carried out with due regard to the need to eliminate unlawful racial discrimination, and to promote 'equality of opportunity, and good relations, between persons of different racial groups'. After the inner city disturbances the Royal Town Planning Institute collaborated with the Commission for Racial Equality to produce a joint report in 1983 on Planning for a Multi-Racial Britain. This recognized that a 'colour-blind' approach to planning may be indirectly discriminatory if it does not recognize cultural diversity and different communities' needs for land and buildings.

> Identical treatment almost guarantees discrimination because people are different in their characteristics, tastes and aspirations. Because people vary and there are differences between races, policies should vary according to differential impact. Uniform treatment is likely to be unequal and may well be unlawful discrimination under the Race Relations Act.
> (RTPI/CRE 1983)

Although the RTPI created an Equal Opportunities (Race) Panel, progress with developing positive guidance for professional practice has been slow. There is an almost complete absence of references to black and ethnic minorities in central government policy guidance. Its guidance (PPG12) on the new-style development plans, published in 1992, was weak on the subject, stating only that:

> 5.48 Authorities will wish to consider the relationship of planning policies and proposals to social needs and problems, including their likely impact on different groups in the population, such as ethnic minorities, elderly and disabled people, single parent families, students, and disadvantaged and deprived people in inner urban areas.
> 5.51 Some authorities may also have other wider social considerations about how they hope to see the social pattern of their communities develop ... The underlying approach must be to limit the plan content to social considerations that are relevant to land-use policies.

A decade after the CRE/RTPI study the RTPI revisited the issue by commissioning a research study on ethnic minorities and the planning system, published in 1993 (Krishnarayan and Thomas 1993). Its terms of reference were:

> To investigate the policies, practices and procedures of planning authorities with large ... ethnic minority populations with a view to assessing:
> (a) the extent to which, and in what ways, attempts are being made to cater for the needs of ethnic minorities;
> (b) the broad implications ... of the adoption of different standards on planning policies, procedures and legislation.

Krishnarayan and Thomas found a variety of approaches, conditioned by local political circumstances, and categorized local planning authorities

into three:
> (a) those regarding race as of no particular relevance to day-to-day planning functions (an attitude encapsulated by the planning nostrum that 'every application is considered on its merits');
> (b) those (perhaps 10 per cent of all LPAs) introducing *ad hoc* innovations, such as employing an ethnic minority liaison officer, in response to perceived problems; and
> (c) a small number prepared seriously to review operating procedures and policies.

They found that London boroughs were becoming more active in the area, with a third monitoring by ethnicity the outcome of at least one of their planning functions.

Krishnarayan and Thomas found some recognition among planners that planning policies can have a disproportionately negative effect on ethnic minority communities. Black businesses operating in the non-retail service sector (e.g. minicab operators and hot-food take-aways) were found to be suffering under planning policies which seek to keep a high proportion of shops in town centres, and protect shop uses generally. Local-level political support was considered important in inducing or encouraging planners to move from a technical approach to a deeper reappraisal of working practice. The study recommended acceptance of two general principles:

> That there is so much evidence of racism in the formulation and implementation of public policy in Britain that the planning system must incorporate features which will alert those involved in it to the possibility of direct or indirect discrimination. Ten years after the RTPI/CRE report there are still a few local authorities which assert that 'there is no problem here', but can point to no systematic evaluation of their planning services which supports this contention.
>
> That it is both unrealistic and unfair to place the entire obligation for securing race equality in town planning onto individual initiatives by professional town planners (or others involved in the planning system). Of course, town planners should combat racial discrimination, but these efforts will be more effective, and more forthcoming, if they are conducted within a supportive framework of legislation, regulation, procedures and advice. The study unearthed a number of well-intentioned individual initiatives which came to nought because of a lack of institutional (including political) support. The study's recommendations focus on feasible measures which if implemented will create a clearer and more positive framework of advice and regulation for undertaking positive action in planning.

The boroughs of inner East London, having some of the highest ethnic minority populations in the country, were by the late 1970s beginning to devise policy guidance for planning applications in those types of development linked to ethnic minorities. Prominent among such policies were those for places of worship and community facilities.

Planning and ethnic minority places of worship

In Spitalfields there is a much-cited symbol of London's history of cultural diversity, and, appropriately for this article, it is a place of religious worship (Jacobs 1996, Wright 1991). Located on the corner of Fournier Street and Brick Lane, the building began as a Huguenot church for the local refugee community of textile weavers in 1744, and subsequently became a Nonconformist chapel for the Wesleyans. With the arrival of Jewish refugees from Eastern Europe it was converted to a Jewish synagogue from 1889 to 1975. In the late nineteenth century the United Synagogue organisation was seeking to make the new Jewish immigrants 'loyal subjects and steadfast Jews', through a building programme of model dwellings, Jewish schools and synagogues (Glasman 1987-8). In the late twentieth century, with the Jewish community largely moved away, the latest wave of immigrants have been the Bangladeshis, and so the building's latest affiliation is to Islam, as a mosque.

The East London Mosque in Whitechapel, designed in brick and with non-functional minarets. Behind is a block of post-war council flats. Photo by Robert Home.

Places of worship for non-western ethnic minorities fulfil an important function as meeting places for their communities, often going beyond the more limited role now associated with most western places of worship. In the early years after arrival in the country the immigrants may adapt premises such as dwelling-houses for worship, and indeed the accustomed western separation between residential and religious use in buildings may not exist. As more funds and other premises become available, purpose-built places of worship may be sought, expressing the status of the community. While freedom of worship is upheld under the Liberty of Religious Worship Act 1855, it has no legal or constitutional guarantee (as specified in the European Convention on Human Rights), and this lack has hampered cases involving religious freedom in legal proceedings, e.g. concerned with employment, education, burial and prisoners' rights (Poulter 1986 and 1990). Obtaining planning permission is another such case, as will be seen.

It would appear that there are approaching two million residents of the United Kingdom who are both ethnic and religious minorities. In 1984 the Registrar-General recorded the following numbers of places of worship in England and Wales certified under the Places of Worship Registration Act 1855 for non-Christian faiths:

JEWS	351
MUSLIMS	290
SIKHS	126
HINDUS	53
BUDDHISTS	18

Certification not being compulsory, these figures will be an under-count, for instance not recording small places of worship in private dwellinghouses. It was estimated in 1984 that there were as many as two thousand mosques and 130 Hindu temples in the United Kingdom (Poulter 1986: 217), and the number of new places of worship has risen in the last decade.

The planning system has slowly come to recognize the need. *Planning for a Multi-Racial Britain* (RTPI/CRE 1983), identified places of worship, burial and cultural assembly as needing particular attention in planning policies. The revision of the Town and Country Planning (Use Classes) Order, undertaken in 1987, put places of religious worship into the Non Residential Institutions Class (D1), in recognition of their social importance, combining teaching, social functions, music, communal eating and advisory services. (The Property Advisory Group, whose investigation had preceded the reform, had recommended including places of worship within an Assembly and Leisure Class, and the RTPI in its representations to the government had argued for a separate or *sui generis* class, but the government considered places of worship to be more akin to public halls and day centres (Home 1989: 67-8).

In practice places of worship for religious minorities can be created in one of three ways: by acquisition from other faiths (as occurred in the Spitalfields case), by conversion of other buildings, and by building new. The latter two would require planning permission. Often quite small premises may be involved, and the communities may be poor, leading to the use of less than ideal properties as a temporary measure. Such premises attract nationally a significant number of enforcement notices (Home, Bloomfield and Maclean 1985).

The planners' professional concern will be, in their particular parlance, how to minimise nuisance and adverse effects upon amenity, in such matters as traffic congestion and parking, noise from the building and people, kitchen smells, and perhaps even funeral preparation. Representations from the public, i.e. the usually predominantly white surrounding population, are often hostile, and NIMBY attitudes ('not in my back yard') are common. One mosque proposal, for example, provoked this revealing reaction from a resident, writing to a local newspaper:

> If the entire Moslem community of Nuneaton were to return to wherever they originated and which has an indigenous Moslem population, the need for this mosque would not exist. The residents who have written to the press and have presented petitions, none of those as usual having any effect, should now if they feel strongly about Islam being thrust down their throats form themselves into an association to raise funds to instruct a solicitor who could in turn instruct Queen's Counsel to apply for an injunction in the Queen's Bench Division of the High Court to restrain the planning authorities from granting a change of use for the site for a purpose which is completely and utterly out of character in this Christian country and in particular in the residential area in question. The legal principle here is that since the residents of Frank Street and Norman Avenue were there first they should have a very strong case. Further if the legal advisers were to give notice to Nuneaton Borough Council, that if this mosque is built they (the residents) will seek a very substantial reduction in the rates they are at present paying, the council would take a lot more notice of the residents' objections than they have done till now.
>
> (Letter in *Evening Tribune* 4 June 1975, supplied to the author by Mohammed Imtiaz, BSc (Land Management) student, UEL 1996).

Policies for places of worship are the commonest ones in development plans that explicitly relate to the needs of the black and ethnic minority population, as Krishnarayan and Thomas (1993) found. Leicester City Council, with a large Asian community, was one of the first local authorities to experiment with such policies (Leicester 1987), and the London Borough of Newham has followed a similarly proactive approach.

Newham has the second highest proportion of ethnic minority residents in the country - some 90,000 people, accounting for 42 per cent of the population. They are also ethnically very diverse, comprising Indians, black Caribbean, Pakistani, black African, Bangladeshi, and a multitude of other nationalities (Sri Lankan, Filipino, Malaysian and Vietnamese), and inter-ethnic tensions can be high (Newham 1990). Of 191 religious/community meeting places listed in the Borough in 1994, 81 per cent were used by Christian faiths, of which over half were used by new Christian faiths for the Afro-Caribbean population. The Borough Planning Department receives a growing number of planning applications for places of worship. Of 94 such applications made between 1984 and 1995, 62 (66 per cent) were granted permission, 10 (10.6 per cent) were refused, and 22 (23.4 per cent) were withdrawn or deferred. The number has been increasing in recent years, as religious groups become more affluent and assertive (Newham 1996).

The Borough accordingly undertook a review of its planning policy framework for community meeting places. This was reported to the Environment and Planning Committee on 6 March 1996, and approved. Its aims were to:

> encourage a more positive partnership between the groups and the surrounding community;
> outline the expected mode of operation following the grant of planning permission; and
> provide a mechanism for the group and neighbouring community to discuss and, hopefully, resolve future concerns that may arise.

The main policy principles were that 'meeting places should be conveniently located to their catchment populations', with former community/public buildings and commercial/industrial premises located outside residential areas being viewed as the most appropriate locations for places of worship. The policy stated that meeting places would normally be supported by the grant of permission, provided that there was no 'significant loss of amenity to adjoining residential uses' and 'associated traffic does not constitute a traffic hazard'. Even in residential areas, places of worship could be allowed where the use was relatively small scale, serving primarily local residents who walk to the facility, but such sites should be 'large enough to accommodate much of the general disturbance associated with the use, so that it would not significantly adversely affect the residential amenity of the area'.

Although East London planning authorities have moved towards a proactive approach, the potential for conflict can slow down the operation of the system, and create practical problems for ethnic minorities in dealing with the planning system and local politics. This is well illustrated by the case which follows, of a Bangladeshi Muslim community's negotiations for a new mosque in Stepney (in which the author was involved as a planning adviser).

Building a Mosque in Stepney

Nearly a quarter (22.9 per cent) of the resident population of the Borough of Tower Hamlets is of Bangladeshi origin (1991 census). During the period of Liberal Democrat control (1986-94), the Borough was divided into seven neighbourhoods, of which Stepney was one. A third of that neighbourhood's resident population (34.5 per cent, 7667 individuals out of 22,245) was Bangladeshi in 1991, and 55.8 per cent were 'white'. Of the Bangladeshi residents 37.9 per cent were born in the United Kingdom.

Black residents were under-represented on the Council. The Globe Town Neighbourhood, for example, had five all-white councillors, although 30 per cent of its heads of household were from ethnic minorities (Thomas and Krisnarayan 1994a). Tenant associations on council housing estates were traditionally run by whites, who had long regarded black immigration as a territorial threat. In the words of Prime Minister Thatcher in 1979, 'Some people have felt swamped by immigrants' (quoted in Thomas 1995: 129). Conflicts between police and black youth on the streets were commonplace. In 1993 the British National Party briefly captured a council seat in a by-election in the Millwall Ward, where the Isle of Dogs white residents were incensed by the allocation of council housing to Bangladeshi families, and Asian voters were intimidated at the polling stations.

Notwithstanding this background, the Borough Plan (Tower Hamlets 1986) expressed the view 'that an understanding of the special needs of racial minorities should run through every policy' (para. 3.42), and a concern that the needs of ethnic minority groups for community facilities should be met (para. 8.73). This was tested when the Bangladeshi community tried to secure a place of worship in Stepney.

The Esha'Atul Islam Foundation was created to serve the religious needs of some three hundred Bangladeshi Muslim families in Stepney, Spitalfields and Brick Lane. The legacy of colonialism had divided the Muslim community of East London. The painful partition of India in 1948 had created

East and West Pakistan, but East Pakistan seceded to become the independent state of Bangladesh in 1971. Attendance at the East London Mosque in Whitechapel led to conflict between Pakistani and Bangladeshi Muslims. The foundation acquired a terraced property at 16 Ford Square in 1983, which it began using as a mosque and madrassa (Koranic school). Then began a decade of disputes and negotiations with the local planning authority.

The use of the building in Ford Square (which lay within a conservation area) soon attracted complaints, and the attention of council enforcement officers. The foundation sought retrospective planning permission for the mosque use in 1986. Although planning applications are statutorily required to be determined within eight weeks, the local planning authority took two years and eight months to consider the application, and then, after vocal local opposition, refused it in 1988. Enforcement action was authorised, but was not proceeded with pending further negotiations.

Wishing to be helpful, the council offered the foundation an adjoining piece of land at the back of the Ford Square premises, which it owned and had intended for public open space. In December 1988, encouraged by the Council, the foundation sought outline planning consent on that land, and it was granted in March 1989, for the development of a mosque, madrassa and cultural centre, at 46/52 Cavell Street and 16 Ford Square, London E1. The outline planning permission reserved a large number of matters for subsequent approval (details of siting, design, external appearance, means of access, landscaping, noise insulation, and disabled access), and prohibited the public call to prayer.

With the security of an outline planning permission the foundation purchased the site from the Council in April 1990, subject to various restrictive covenants, including one limiting the use of the site to an 'Islamic Mosque'. The site was small for its purpose, and a gross floor area of 1500 sq.m. on a site of 658 sq.m. was proposed, requiring a building of three storeys.

There then followed yet more years of delay and haggling over design details. Details of siting and means of access were approved in June 1990, and various meetings and discussions with Council officers led to a further application for the remaining reserved matters in September 1991. This initially showed an increase in floorspace, but was redesigned down to the originally approved size. There were further meetings between the applicants' agents and Council officers, and various letters were exchanged, and revised drawings submitted. The new application was first reported to the Neighbourhood Committee in July 1992, but deferred for a committee members' site meeting, which did not occur until October. At the site meeting the committee expressed various concerns, in response to which yet more design revisions were made, all lessening the visual effect of the building as a mosque. These involved:

(a) removal of the minaret originally proposed. A prohibition on the call to prayer had already been imposed in both the deeds and condition on the outline consent, so that any minaret would be of symbolic significance only.
(b) reduction of the height of the main and subordinate domes, making the dome feature associated with mosques almost invisible.
(c) modifications to window details, reducing the Islamic ornamentation proposed.
(d) alteration of the facing materials from marble to Indiana limestone (at a substantially higher cost).
(e) enlargement of the entrance lobby.

Many letters of objection to the application had been received, mostly from white residents of the neighbourhood council housing estate, regarding likely noise, disturbance and the principle of a mosque use at all (even though that had been conceded in the outline permission). While the sale of the land for the mosque had been authorized by a Labour majority, by now the Stepney neighbourhood was Liberal Democrat controlled, and the local Liberal Democrat party was under severe local pressure from racist political organizations, notably the British National Party. The local party's promotional literature was criticized in the national press for pandering to racism, and the national party had to intervene to ensure compliance with party policy against racial discrimination.

The revised application came before the neighbourhood committee on 9 December 1992. In spite of an officers' recommendation of approval, it was turned down. The sole reason for refusal - a rather flimsy one in planning terms - was that: 'the design and external appearance of the proposed new building would be out of character, unsympathetic, and not in keeping with the surrounding buildings and area in general, which lies on the edge of a conservation area'.

The foundation was now in the position of owning a site which it had bought from the council under a restrictive covenant that the land be occupied only by a mosque, but which it could not develop for that purpose because that same council would not grant planning permission. The foundation immediately exercised its statutory right of appeal to central government (the Secretary of State for the Environment).

Subjected to all these frustrations, and still short of space, the foundation erected a temporary portakabin on the mosque site, but the council objected and it was removed shortly before the detailed planning application was reported to committee, so as not to prejudice that matter. After the refusal, the foundation erected a temporary prayer hall on the otherwise vacant appeal site, considering that the outline permission gave it at least that right. In April 1993 the Council resolved to serve an enforcement notice for its removal, giving as reasons for service that the structure 'detracts from the visual amenities of the area' and an 'over intensification of use'. The notice was not served, so as not to inflame the situation pending the outcome of the appeal.

The appeal (Department of Environment reference APP/E5900/A/93/217172) was heard at a one-day public local inquiry on 4 November 1993 in the Stepney Neighbourhood Offices. Both sides used barristers as advocates, and the appellants called one witness on planning and one on design. In spite of the many letters of objection to the application, none of the local residents (apart from the foundation members) attended the inquiry, and fears of racist demonstrations were not realized.

Much of the evidence at the inquiry concerned the character of the surrounding area. The Council claimed that the mosque site lay 'in the middle of a built up area with distinctive architectural and building traditions'. These distinctive traditions in practice were no more than the mixture of building type, period and use typical of an inner city area. The mosque site was located between the A11 and A13 trunk roads, immediately east of the London Hospital, and much of the surrounding area had been redeveloped since World War Two, predominantly for council housing. The site itself was bounded by two multi-storey brick-built factories (built in the early twentieth century), a four-storey block of deck-access council housing (from which came many of the letters of objection), and a public garden with benches and semi-mature trees. The rest of Cavell Street was in mixed use, comprising three and four storey flats, garment-making factories, corner shops, cafés and offices. Many of the businesses and residents in the immediate area were Bangladeshi by origin.

Although the reason for refusal referred to the nearby Sidney Square Conservation Area, the mosque site could only be seen indirectly from one corner of it. The value of the conservation area was in any case debatable, since less than half of it contained older buildings, mostly modest three- and four-storeyed nineteenth-century terraced housing. The rest of it (at the time of designation) comprised vacant sites awaiting redevelopment, and it appears that a major objective of the Council in designating the area was to secure more control over the design of new development. Most of the sites were subsequently redeveloped for housing during the late 1980s, using pastiche designs that echoed the style of the surviving 19th century terraces.

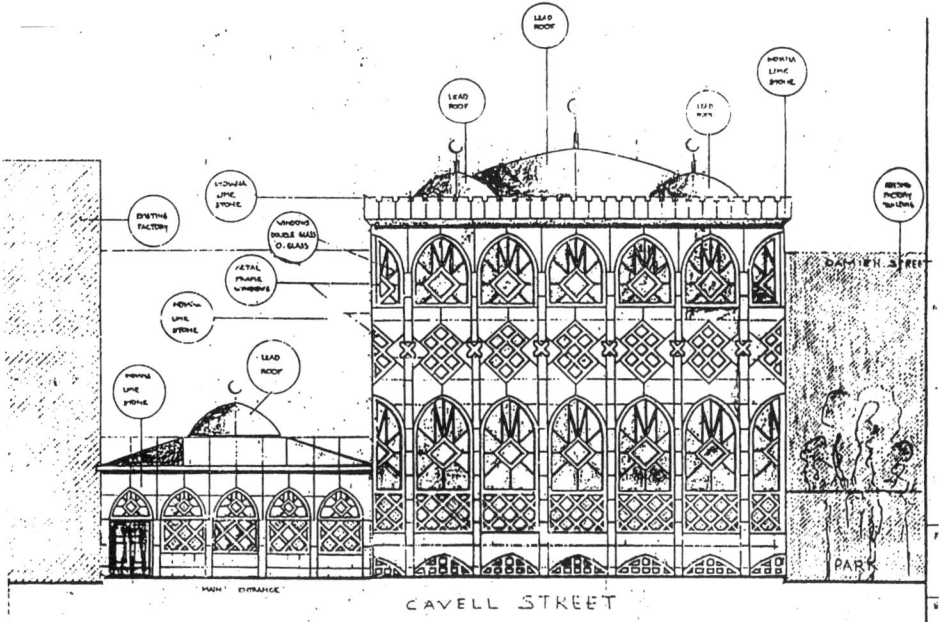

The planning expert witness for the foundation said that one would expect a mosque by its very nature to include a dome, minaret, large windows in geometric pattern, and high-quality exterior cladding, within the Islamic traditions. In this case the council had chosen to object to practically every aspect of the detailed application which would identify the building as a mosque. To accommodate the council's argument that a predominance of brick and simplicity of detail in the adjoining buildings should be reflected in the mosque design, the foundation's architect even went to the lengths of producing a totally revised scheme in brick, which removed all design features of a mosque, and looked like a block

Above: Design for the new mosque at Cavell Street: no minarets, and domes so flattened they almost lose their role in an attempt to fit into the area.
Below: Design for the new mosque at Cavell Street: a brick and slate alternative in response to the planners.

of flats, but this design was not put forward at the inquiry as an alternative.

The Bangladeshis won their appeal. The inspector's four-page decision letter, of 3 December 1993, found that the appearance of the Conservation Area would be positively enhanced by the proposed development:

> While the style of building may be unusual and the degree of ornamentation considerably greater than was shown in the original outline sketches, Annex A of Planning Policy Guidance Note 1 'General Policy and Principles' acknowledges that aesthetic judgements are to some extent subjective, and states that authorities should not impose their taste on applicants simply because they believe it to be superior. The appeal scheme is architect designed, and enjoyed the support of the council's professional officers, including its Historic Buildings Officer. It would provide for a distinctive building constructed from good quality materials, which would complement the wide range of colours and textures employed in other buildings throughout the area. It would also contribute to the diversity of cultural and religious facilities which have long typified the rich social history of this part of London. In my judgement, there would be no serious conflict with the prevailing planning policies, and the scheme would have no adverse effect on the character and appearance of the area.

While vindicating the appellants, the Inspector was shy of confronting the issue of racial discrimination. The planning expert witness for the foundation had concluded that the application was refused for reasons of racial discrimination rather than planning, and this formed the basis of a claim for costs at the inquiry. The inspector, in deciding the claim, made no specific reference to racial discrimination, confining himself to the more cautious statement:

> You contended that Council Members had been swayed by unfounded opposition to the scheme from a substantial body of local residents who did not accept that the principle of a mosque and madrasah on the site had been established by the permission granted in 1988.

He dismissed the claim for costs in the following words:

> While I understand your client's frustration in being unable to achieve a scheme which met with the Council's approval, I see nothing in the evidence before me which suggests that the Council's opposition was based on anything other than concern for the quality of the built environment.

Armed at last with their permission, after a ten year battle for the right to worship in the area, the foundation was in a position to build its mosque.

CONCLUSIONS

The urban landscape of East London is affected by a condition of postcolonialism, in which new communities created by the process of decolonization of Britain's overseas empire have to contest with the dominant culture for a share of the built environment. The struggle of ethnic minorities to establish their own places for worship and community meeting illustrates how conflicting claims upon the urban landscape are mediated through the land use planning system.

Planning policy, ostensibly operating through a professional-technical system that was 'colour-blind', can often serve to sustain and reproduce a built environment that is inimical to black and ethnic minorities. A Conservative central government committed to a free market ideology had little interest in positive interventions on behalf of ethnic minorities, as its consistently weak policy guidance shows. The planning professional institute, while willing to commission research which came to some fairly robust conclusions, remained reluctant to consolidate those findings into firm guidance on policy and practice.

The local planning authorities of East London have gradually acknowledged the needs of ethnic minorities through supportive wording in local planning policies, but these also allowed local discretion. The conflicts inherent in proposals for ethnic minority places of worship have resulted in an uncertain and slow response by the planning system. Local politicians' perceptions of the communities that they should serve, and pressures from rival political groups, have sometimes led them into conflict with their own officers. In the case of the Stepney mosque the neighbourhood councillors responded to local white opposition and thwarted for a decade the aspirations of the ethnic minority community, until central government intervention was required through the planning appeal system.

While the Bangladeshi Muslim organization as developer was eventually successful, the underlying postcolonialist tensions were submerged in a decision framed in the quasi-technical language of the planning professional. A rhetoric designed around planning concepts of conservation and amenity was the language of discourse at the planning inquiry and in the decision letter, in preference to one which made explicit the issues of racial and community conflict.

The author wishes to acknowledge the help of the following: Ali Shauquat, Ram Aurora, Tim Butler, Phil Cohen, Mohammed Imtiaz, Simon Pattle, and Dilbagh Virdee.

REFERENCES

Cohen, P., Tarek Qureshi and Toon, I., *Island Stories: Race, class and ethnicity in the remaking of east enders*, University of East London, New Ethnicities Unit, London 1993.

Cohen, P., *Towards a Multi-cultural University*, University of East London, New Ethnicities Unit, London 1995.

Cooper, J., and Tarek Qureshi, *Through Patterns not our Own: a study of the regulation of racial violence on the council estates of East London*, University of East London, New Ethnities Research and Education Group, London 1993.

CRE, *Roots of the Future: ethnic diversity in the making of Britain*, Commission for Racial Equality, 1996.

Cullingworth Report, *Council Housing: Purposes, Procedures and Priorities*, Ministry of Housing and Local Government, HMSO, London 1969.

Fryer, P., *Staying Power: The history of black people in Britain*, Pluto Press, London 1984.

Glasman, J., 'London Synagogues in the late Nineteenth Century: Design in Context.', *London Journal*, Number 13, Volume 2, pp143-55.

Home, R., J.Bloomfield and N.Maclean, 'Trends in enforcement appeals', *Estates Gazette*, Number 276, pp266-76.

Home, R.K., *Planning Use Classes*, Blackwell Scientific (2nd edition), Oxford 1989.

Husbands, C., 'East End racism, 1900-1980: geographical continuities in vigilantism and extreme right wing political behaviour', *London Journal*, Volume 1, Number VIII, pp3-26.

Jackson, P., *Maps of Meaning: An introduction to cultural geography*, Unwin Hyman, London 1989.

Jacobs, J.M., *Edge of Empire: postcolonialism and the city*, Routledge, London 1996.

Krishnarayan, V. and Thomas, H., *Ethnic Minorities and the Planning System*, Royal Town Planning Institute, London 1993.

Leicester, *Places of Worship in Leicester*, Report of Working Party, City Planning Department, Leicester 1987.

Memon, P.A., 'Public policy in an ethnically plural society', *Town Planning Review*, Volume 11, Number 59, 1988, pp45-63.

Merriman, N. (ed), *The Peopling of London*, Museum of London, London 1993.

NFHA, *Accommodating Diversity: the design of housing for minority ethnic, religious and cultural groups*, National Federation of Housing Associations, London 1993.

Newham, *Newham: The forging of a black community*, Newham Monitoring Project: Campaign Against Racism and Fascism, London 1991.

Newham, *Review of planning policy framework for community meeting places*, London Borough of Newham Planning Department, London 1996.

Poulter, S., *English Law and Ethnic Minority Customs*, Butterworth, London 1986.

Poulter, S., *Asian Traditions and English Law: A Handbook*, Runnymede Trust with Trentham Books, London 1990.

PPG12, *Development Plans*, Department of the Environment, Planning Policy Guidance, London 1992.

Rex, J., *Race, Colonialism and the City*, Routledge & Kegan Paul, London 1973.

Rhodes, C. and N.Nabi, 'Brick Lane: a village economy in the shadow of the city?' in L.Budd and S.Whimster (eds), *Global Finance and Urban Living*, Routledge, London 1992, pp33-52.

RTPI/CRE, *Planning for a Multi-racial Britain*, Royal Town Planning Institute and Commission for Racial Equality, London 1983.

Thomas, H., '"Race", public policy and planning in Britain', *Planning Perspectives*, Volume 2, Number 10, 1995, pp123-48.

Thomas, H., and V. Krishnarayan, 'Race and planning in London: A contemporary view', *Cities*, Volume 11, Number 4, 1994a, pp264-71.

Thomas, H., and V.Krishnarayan (eds), *Race equality and planning: policies and procedures*, Ashgate, Aldershot 1994b.

Tower Hamlets, *Adopted Borough Development Plan*, London Borough of Tower Hamlets, 1986.

Wright, P., *A Journey Through Ruins: The Last Days of London*, Radius Press, London 1991.

Race and Place in 'Schizophrenic' Narratives [1]

Caroline Knowles shows how black activists have managed to reorganize parts at least of the community mental health system in East London and have created several black centres devoted to meeting the needs of black people diagnosed as mentally ill. She shows how this has become a complex medley of provision in which black patients often visit a number of centres or else choose one that meets their particular definitions of themselves. She concludes that despite the success of black people in 'racializing community space', this has been limited by the organization of the system which 'works against the needs of its users'. She suggests that more fundamental and racially articulate reforms are necessary to address the needs of those forced to use the system.

PLACES ARE PHYSICAL and territorial, conceptual and symbolic, invested with social meaning and linked by the ways in which lives and administrative actions are cast. Places are about the social relationships which constitute them as much as they are about conceptual or physical territory. Never neutral, places are highly racialized (Cohen 1996:71): race is a liminal part of the symbolic meaning of place. In the spatialized vocabularies of social theory there is a growing awareness that 'Places ... constitute the sentient individual': that there is a relationship between identity and the spaces through which it is produced and expressed (Keith and Pile 1993:9), a point which is convincingly empirically demonstrated by Cohen (1996). This paper describes the processes by which certain places, places making up the community of the community mental health care system, are organized as racialized productions.[2] The community of the community mental health care system catering to 'black'.[3] East Londoners is the product of a dialogue between black political activists concerned with mental health, psychiatric practice, local community work, a particular local way of administering the mentally distressed, a way of seeing schizophrenia and the lives and views of those who use the system.[4] There are a number of versions of black schizophrenic life in play each with its own conception of the place which is the community of the community mental health care system. Places, and their racialized social relationships then, are multi-dimensioned and contested. Users of community services cast the existential project of the self in negotiating others' conceptions of their identity and their symbolic place in the locale. The resulting system of community provision is not as dominated by the hegemonic power of formal psychiatry as its critics have suggested: it is rather a set of inadequate and inappropriate resources organized with enthusiasm and dedication, and used in creative and unpredictable ways.

Dialogues with administrative conceptions

The spaces comprising the community mental health services of East London are generated in a complex dialogue. This paper shows how each of the players in this dialogue generate their own versions of blackness and schizophrenia. These players have essentially different qualities. Psychiatry and community care are administrative systems whose notions of personhood are fashioned by the fact that they have to deal with the mentally distressed. Psychiatric patients and users of the system, on the other hand, operate around existential conceptions of the self. The self is not unproblematic. It involves interpreting what is said, acted or lived; a recollective project in which we explore life histories from the vantage point of the present (Freeman 1993:4,36). The self is not a thing, but a selective and imaginary interpretation of the words and actions used to speak about lives (Freeman 1993:6-8). The self in the narratives of our psychiatric patient informants is contextualized through three key themes: the meaning and phenomenology of the 'problem' and its place in the life story; the use of community resources; and the prospect of reconnection with some other community outside of the system. In the dialogue between the self and the administrative, the project of understanding blackness as schizophrenia is cast, and with it the nature of the place occupied by East London's community mental health services.

NAMING AND EXPLAINING

The conceptualization of schizophrenia and the therapeutic strategies for dealing with it are embedded in the diverse narratives of psychiatry. Schizophrenia is variously located in the ecology of the human brain, in social interactions, in family history (identified by Laing) and in the loss of selfhood (identified by Winnicott) (Barham 1984:95). Barham (1984:21) suggests that if one examines the dominant social construction of schizophrenia within psychiatry we are looking at the emergence of a disease entity which is chronic and incurable, and at the identification of the schizophrenic as a social type. The modalities of clinical management (because there is no cure) for schizophrenia have a particular form in community mental health care, the key strategies of which are best described in the testimonies of schizophrenics themselves as domains of experience. Describing schizophrenia through the life world of the schizophrenic, subjects formal psychiatry's chronicity, incurability and pharmacological management to critical scrutiny; but at the same time raises doubts concerning the extent to which we are relying on delusional texts for our critique. Most of the stories we collected were not recognizably part of a delusion, but they were spoken through the filters of psychotropic medication. But even if the life world of the schizophrenic is delusional, delusions have a phenomenology rather than raise issues of reality (Lacan 1993:34,77), and schizophrenics (if that is indeed what they are) are productive and useful agents of history who make sense of their own lives (Barham 1984:2) and who give useful and original testimony (Lacan 1993:208).

The chronicity of schizophrenia as well as the notion of the schizophrenic as a social type are contested in the narratives of schizophrenics themselves who stress the theme of reconnection. The idea of reconnection with another community outside of the system marks the system as a definite space which is entered and vacated with the rhythms of episodes of distress, and offers the prospect of resuming a former life. A key reconnective strategy is the demonstration of wellness, a project in which interviews with informants are often enlisted as a chance to perform wellness for anyone who is watching.[5]

Psychiatry organizes the naming of pathology, something which system users variously concur with or contest.

> 'They [who improperly understood who Don was or how he got ill] called it schizophrenia'. I saw a doctor in ... hospital and I talked to him and I told him why and how I felt and he said to me 'do you smoke drugs?' and I said 'yeah I smoke cannabis' and he said 'Well I know the solution to your problem, oh I know the solution'. As if it's been drugs and that wasn't the solution at all. But that's how they think. I mean if you go into hospital for any reason and you've been in a situation and its similar to the people they've treated before...they said 'okay you need what we've given them'. No they don't treat you individually, they just treat you like, this is the drug you're going to be put on because you said this, yeah.

Terry, perhaps picking up on schizophrenia's incurability, saw the fact that he felt well as evidence of misdiagnosis, a popular theme among psychiatry's critics.

> No, they said it was schizophrenia but it wasn't, I'm not one of them though, cause I've been discharged as not mentally ill now, so I'm not schizophrenic that's for sure, I'm not but that's what they said it was anyways, that's what we're treating.

Although they had to negotiate schizophrenia as a naming of themselves by others, our informants were naturally less concerned with naming and matching diagnoses with behaviour than they were with explaining what was wrong, what had caused it and its overall place in their life story. Their accounts of causes mirror the divergence in psychiatry between biologically and socially based explanations.[6] They describe as a journey their decline from normality to mental distress and the social relationships and events surrounding what they saw as the moment(s) of crisis. These moments were either sudden or worked-up; involved their complicity or happened to them. For Jon schizophrenia happened to him, suddenly, with the onset of the 'voices':

> It just comes...I was on an electronics course when it happened...It was terrible, it was like I heard loads of voices, like they were after me and it was like a mob, lots of people shouting. There was no one there...I must have over studied or something like that...I was using my mind too much.

Jon's explanation partly absorbs the psychiatric explanation that his mind is the site of the problem, to which he adds his own, that it blows rather like an electric circuit when overloaded. Both the mind and its circuitry are beyond his control and properly belong to the domain of professionals. Don, on the other hand, explains his journey into the 'mental institute' as a more gradual process which he works on for two years during which time he speaks to no-one and reads the Bible.

> After those two years I was ill I walked out on the streets and I met a policeman. I was doing some very strange things at that time. I met a policeman and I was in his way and he said to me if I don't move he's going to arrest me, and I said to him 'If you touch me I'm going to punch you in the face'. And he did exactly what he said he was going to do and I did exactly what I said I was going to do....I looked like a mad man...people looked at me like I was a mad man...I went mad because I had nowhere to live...They (friends) saw me in a different way and I saw them in a different way...I started to hallucinate not because of the drugs, it was me myself, forcing myself to hallucinate because I wanted to see life in a better light. I saw the stars, I tell you one time, I ... you know those birds that deliver babies? ... I never saw one of those before ... To be quite honest with you

[asked to reflect on the causes of schizophrenia], what they need is a bit of happiness in their lives, to take them away from their problems ... what I needed was a place of my own, help to fix it up, a job.

In telling his story of who he is and what his illness means, Don is forced to deal with the fact that others see him as mad. Schizophrenia for him, as for many of the people we spoke to, is the denial of a route into citizenship through a job, home, family and friendships; and its symptoms, the delusions, are a conscious means of escape from a life which lacks these qualities.

THERAPEUTIC STRATEGIES: MEDICATION AND HOSPITALISATION

Psychiatry organises the treatment of the pathologies it identifies. Hospitalisation is now a minimal feature of the local East London psychiatric system which operates through short hospital stays to deal with crises, and the long-term management of patients in the community. From an administrative standpoint 'crises' are stabilised with medication and 'patients' released on the basis of their ability to function outside of the hospital: a calculation which is often at odds with users' notions of well-being and need for asylum. Users' assessments of the local psychiatric wards focus on how well they meet the need for temporary retreat; the behaviour of the (nursing) staff towards them, especially how well they were listen to, understood and treated; and the quality of the social relationships between patients. Paul for example thought hospital 'was good', it made him 'better' because 'all the doctors and nurses are there to help me'. Don, on the other hand, thought the staff had favourites preferring 'loud mouths' that could 'convince them that they really are ill and that they really belong there...I don't belong there but I need help'.[7] Referring to one of North East London's major psychiatric facilities he told us:

> I was just asleep and I woke up, sat down with the other patients, had cigarettes, ate the food. That was all I was doing...It was horrible. It's inhumane the way they treat you and the drugs they give you, sometimes they ain't even the right drugs. I think that hospital should be closed as soon as possible. There's a lot of people suffering up there [in the secure unit]....I was stuck in a room where I couldn't leave. That's not the environment for someone that's ill. Imagine being stuck in a room. I mean in a bleak room and there's a TV. No video. No music...You've just lost your freedom, that's all you've done. And you're not going to get better. The only way to get better is for the doctors to say 'okay it's about time we reduce the medication'...I tell you one thing, it was worse than being in prison. When I was in prison, I knew there was no way out until my time

had come, but in hospital you didn't know where you were going. You could be there, you could come out tomorrow or you could be in there for ever.

For Audrey, who has twelve children and believes that god makes her ill when she 'does bad things', the local psychiatric wards were a refuge:

> I call it a rest because sometimes I book myself into the hospital. When I say I book myself, I don't act strange or get out of order, it's just that I tend to want to get away...I don't know if some people are in hospital because they want someone to look after them for a while. You know when you want to get up, have your breakfast and just walk about, where someone's looking after you - without medication. I don't want medication, I just want someone to be there, like at breakfast, at lunch and dinner, and that's what they put me into, you know, in taking away the children (and hence her claim to housing) and letting me be put on the road. I don't want to go back into society, being a mum any more, you know.

Hospitalisation was not a situation Audrey initiated, but one she is making the best of. Psychiatric wards may be poor people's only chance of a rest-cure.

Both hospital and community manage schizophrenia through psychotropic medication administered in the community in the form of regular injections by psychiatric nurses and GPs under the formal direction of psychiatrists: the source of most complaints voiced by our informants. Don describes the effects of the drugs as an alarming experience.

> My fingers wouldn't work no more...everything ceases up...And I was like a spastic, and I couldn't walk, my speech was blurred and my tongue...it made me dribble and I was looking pathetic, but these are the drugs they say work, but it doesn't work on all people...it scared me. I thought I was going to be maimed for life.

Drugs, we learned, create the schizophrenic lifestyle and the schizophrenic 'look'. They curtail social interaction and activity, induce feelings of lethargy, produce swelling tongues and dry mouths which make speech difficult, they create stiff necks and the obesity which comes with reduced activity and community centre life. Most aware of this was Amir, who went to great lengths to control his body shape through borderline anorexic behaviour. The visible signs of madness, then, are generated by the treatment and not the problem. Although they were unpopular the drugs controlled the voices and the hallucinations: overall the consequences of not taking them were more terrifying than their side-effects. Terry, who thought the drugs worked by sorting-out the brain, the site of the 'problem', told us drugs were anyway not a matter for negotiation. 'You're not allowed to say no to the medication. What's written-up for you is yours.'

The conceptualisation and treatment of schizophrenia plays a major part in the organisation of place in community psychiatric services of East London: a place which can only be understood through the administrative and existential dialogues in which it is constituted. Schizophrenic lives are produced as much by the social agency of those who live them, as by the administrative actions of psychiatry. The uniqueness of East London lies precisely in this combination of the administrative and the existential. The general administrative features of schizophrenia are similar throughout London and the United Kingdom with small regional variations linked with the policies and practices of Area Health Authorities and Mental Health Trusts. It is in the processing of the administrative by the local black schizophrenic population that the special character of East London is found.

Community mental health services in East London

With the revolving doors of the local psychiatric wards standing-in for the old asylums of the area, the effective jurisdiction of formal psychiatry is now a minimal part of modern psychiatric care. Given this shift, critiques locating the racialized practices of psychiatry need to refocus on the social and spatial relationships of the community. It is the community of the community psychiatric care system in East London and the means by which it is racialized which is the focus of the rest of this paper.

The community in which community mental health care is positioned in East London has some special characteristics as well as features which it shares with other places. As Cohen (1996:178) points out, the East End carries a massive burden of representation: it is historically the site of multiple imagining, social anxiety and social reform. It has a special place in the conceptual schemas of researchers especially those concerned with race. My own research, which began in the mid-1970s with the investigation of local Labour Parties' approaches to race and community, has never quite managed to leave the area, although I have relocated twice, once to live and work in West Africa and then, later, to Quebec. Although moving from one empirical dimension of racialization (political discourse) to another (psychiatry), I mine the same locale for intellectual insight. As a conceptual place the East End of London is a special place in the imagining of social researchers.

It also has some special dimensions as a territory, not least because of its demographic diversity and links with racialization. The East End is a place of great population mobility with white (flight) outward migration and inward migration from populations born outside of the UK. In Hackney, Tower Hamlets and Waltham Forest in particular, about one quarter to a third of the population is born outside of Britain and the majority come from non-white ethnic groups (Rix 1996:24). In Tower Hamlets one quarter of all residents are of Indian, Pakistani or Bangladeshi origin (Rix 1996:28), with a substantial number of refugees from Sri Lanka and Somalia and other African countries (Bloch 1996:156). The racial demographics of the East End vary enormously; in Waltham Forest, for example, a quarter of the population is non-white and this is equally divided between Asians and African Caribbeans (Rix 1996:29). An area of considerable racial tension, issues in the East End are readily seen in racial terms, and not infrequently as turf battles between racially construed groups. Some East End boroughs also claim high levels of mental ill health on the grounds that the mentally ill migrate to the inner city (Hackney Schizophrenia Guide 1993); and, an additional and related issue is the high and rapidly expanding homeless population of the area (Rix 1996:29).

The research project on which this paper is based is a comparative one. Part of it is based in Montreal where there are no special black spaces in mental health care provision; the other part involved interviewing in day centres, hostels and black projects in the East London areas of Tower Hamlets, Bow, Bethnal Green and Waltham Forest. There were, however, generally no substantial differences to the findings in these centres and of those in Islington, Lambeth, Haringey, Borough and Lewisham. Key differences between East London and other parts of London are to do with the precise networks connecting Area Health Authorities, Mental Health Trusts, local Social Services and the linking of mental health care delivery systems with broader aspects of patient well-being, in addition to the local elements evident in individual biographies. Community mental health care is the place where the discrete budgetary turfs of Mental Health Trusts and their internal markets (which still largely provide according to 'need'), meet the discretionary and highly rationed resources of local Social Services. This is a cash-starved system in which geographical notions of place are connected by administrative networks. The division between a patient's mental health and care needs is an artificially one. The result is that users of the system often fall between two administrative networks and two budgets.[8]

This community is not only a conceptual and geographical site, it is a set of social relationships (Barham 1984:178) positioned within a shifting sense of place. This article attempts to describe some of the social relationships and mobile sense of locale which make up community mental health care in East London. This community plays a specific part in psychiatry's revolving door circuit. It is positioned between hospital and the other (symbolic or metaphoric), but no less real, community (Keith & Pile 1993:23) in which people who are not mentally distressed live more self-sufficient lives which are not administered by psychiatry but by other systems. Both the community of psychiatric care and the 'other' community are, of course, representations of processes arrested by moments of arbitrary closure (Keith and Pile 1993:28). What follows is an attempt to examine some of the moments which constitute these processes.

The circuit connecting psychiatric wards, the community of community mental health care and the other community of greater self-sufficiency works like this. Short hospital stays are followed by temporary accommodation in the dormitories of hostels and partially sheltered (assisted) accommodation whose operational units are 'bed spaces'. These give way to half-way houses offering some assistance and crash courses on self-sufficiency (or how to join the other community). These temporary arrangements in turn give way to other temporary arrangements: flats, bedsits or spare rooms loaned by friends and relatives supplemented by the 'day fillers' of the (day) centres. The next relapse sets this tenuous circuit in motion again with a hospital admission. Many of the people we spoke to had been round this circuit on a yearly or even twice yearly basis. The chronically mentally distressed, by virtue of the organization of community care, lead highly mobile lives. They are psychiatric system nomads: part of a shifting mass whose job and housing prospects are circumscribed by the mobility which comes with the management of chronic mental distress.

Community mental health care consists of a series of loosely connected and broadly geographically based *ad hoc* networks of community centres, hostels, projects, programmes of activities and sheltered housing; some of which specialize in mental health and some of which is multi-purpose, serving a more broadly defined set of community needs from mothers and toddlers groups to alternative healing and yoga. Informal community care is often a series of bolt-on parts which have a temporary feel and which are sensitive to the fluctuations of public funding and charitable donations. Some centres have an institutional or municipal appearance, announcing themselves with signs on the door;[9] others fade into the housing stock on the street, their purpose unannounced. The physical state of the buildings and their facilities varies enormously, but most are fairly dilapidated and run down even 'squat-like' in appearance with a feeling of temporariness reflecting the situation of the users. Other centres managed - through a highly structured programme of activities - to give a greater sense of permanence, and some (clearly better resourced) were well-maintained and furnished. Staff who were generally dedicated and hard working, predominantly black and female, with high turn-over and burn-out rates, led professional lives which mirrored the temporaries of the lives of centre-users.

Centres commonly live in various states of racial tension with the other residents and users of the locales in which they are situated. Space is dominated by different sets of meanings: the symbolism of landscape is always malleable and subject to active contestation (Keith and Pile 1993:25). There were fears about safety on both sides with residents petitioning local councillors on the dangers posed by madness threatening the safety of 'neighbourhood' life. Centre-users on the other hand feared the consequences of being unwelcome and, especially, racial harassment and physical attack. When one of the centres in which we were interviewing was the object of an arson attack this was interpreted by some of its users as a sign of local hostility and by others as revenge by a past centre-user. Local issues, residence and use, in the areas in which the centres are located are readily construed in racial terms, and the racial topography of locale clearly effects the ways in which the centres are perceived with madness adding another layer of dangerousness to blackness.

Centres are shaped by their internal management of space, activities and users; processes in which staff and general ethos play a significant part. Some centres allow users to casually drift in and out with others controlling access to buildings so as to allow a monitoring of arrivals and departures with entry phones. Some offer minimally differentiated hanging-out space: lounges offering television and coffee. Others have clearly marked-out internal spaces - reading room, dining area, meeting rooms - with time spent in more structured ways around organized activities. Activities (group meetings, typing skills, art and crafts) are either internally resourced or use local community resources such as swimming pools and other community centres which offer more specialized activities such as music. Centres using the 'outside' commonly escort their users (like minors) in minibuses and staff cars in ways which are quite enfeebling. Different activities have different values and meanings attached to them, some being more central than others. In one centre the music club had a high status and was colonized by its most visible users. In some centres subsidized and good quality lunches were a central focus of the day: staying for lunch was both a sign of membership and a reward for participation. But these activities were not neutral, they were culturally marked by the kinds of food and music they served, with their own forms of inclusion and exclusion.

SOCIAL RELATIONSHIPS

One of the most significant dynamics in the social relations of community mental health spaces is between users, and between users and workers. Those who share living space engage in noticeable power-plays. The currencies of internal contestation of space concern who chooses the videos, who controls the TV, who is the loudest, and who dominates the central spaces and activities. Threat, encroachment on the spaces occupied by others, offering alternative spaces to the centre, gentleness, generosity, visibility, invisibility and loudness were some of the strategies through which users occupied their centre and positioned themselves in relation to each other and the workers. Des, for example, was powerful because he offered an alternative to the centre by gathering around himself a group of younger men living at home with their mothers whom he allows to go to his flat to drink and meet women. Displays of excess and sexual prowess (disallowed by centres) were highly significant as ways of establishing and servicing the centre identities of users, and the social relationships through which they were construed. There are other strategies too through which users position themselves in centres. Amir's mint green leggings and silver body-warmer along with his anorexic body mark him out in the drab institutional surroundings which contextualize his life, and re-align him with another life on the street outside. Jane on the other hand doesn't want to attract attention to herself or get in anyone's way. She is undemanding, disciplined, stays close to the office and interacts primarily with the workers: a model user of this particular centre, she is invisible.

Access, activities, and the social relationships, ethos and political consciousness of centres all construe a particular (administrative) version of the user. Whilst this varied quite a bit there were some common themes. Users were younger (under 40), predominantly male (with spaces for women being clearly marked by female staff and more traditionally feminine activities such as sewing, yoga and word processing), fit a particular version of blackness and bring a specific range of experiences of mental distress and the systems managing it. This administrative version of the user generated its own comfort zone in which certain users, with an appropriate biography, and not others would more easily be able to operate. It was not clear whether centres exercised more direct forms of exclusion than this. In one centre a worker tried to stop us interviewing Nigel because he was 'subnormal' and therefore 'wouldn't fit the study'. Nigel didn't fit the centre either, but he'd been there for years before it became a consciously black space in the way it was now. He had not been eased-out by the comfort zone, and no-one wanted to actually exclude him. Nigel was black but he was not 'mad' in the right kind of way. Centres had their own exclusionary mechanisms and their own ideas about our research which, though generally approved-of as socially useful, was closely monitored in one particular centre by the head of the users group who controlled who we could speak to and hence the range of narratives we had access to.

Racialization of community mental health care

The spaces comprising community mental health care are carefully managed racialized productions. Race is liminal: it is a fundamental organizing principle of social life in the area and a set of context specific repertoires (Winant 1994:267-268). It is simultaneously a significant dimension of both individual and collective identities. It is part of how we see ourselves and how we are seen by others. Seeing ourselves (the existential) and being seen (the cultural and administrative) in racialized terms are quite different dimensions of identity. Race as blackness invokes a collective identity, a naming, associated with various dimensions of incapacity and social disadvantage (racism): and it invokes the contestation of that naming and disadvantage (anti-racism). Race then is local, contextual, individual, collective, dialogically generated and symbolically organized. In the circumstances under consideration it is organized within the administrative framework of East End community mental health care and its appropriate symbols, agents and forms of contestation. What follows is a description of the mechanisms by which the community of community mental health care is racialized.

POLITICAL PRESSURE

The gradual creation, since the 1980s, of black spaces in community mental health care may be seen as a symbolic political gesture responding to a range of concerns expressed by community activists, a vociferous (though white-dominated) survivors' movement, psychiatrists and academics, about the ways in which black psychiatric patients are managed by the system. Mounting evidence that black, and specifically African-Caribbean, patients were overdiagnosed with serious and chronic disorders, especially schizophrenia; misunderstood and inappropriately dealt with (Littlewood and Lipsedge 1988, Littlewood 1993, Francis 1989, Sashidharan 1992) provided the political impetus for reform. The heavy-handed treatment of black patients by the police and psychiatric staff as they accessed the system, their concentration on locked wards and their management through compulsory sections of the Mental Health Act, presaged a widespread recognition that the mental health care system's management of blackness presented an urgent problem to be addressed. The issue of whether they were 'really' schizophrenic is less significant than critics of psychiatry have claimed: and to assert this as a central issue is to give undue weight to the diagnostic strategies of formal psychiatry rather than to understanding the lives of those who are so labelled.[10]

ORGANIZATIONAL STRUCTURES

A number of organizational structures, priorities and provisions developed in response to the system's handling of race and these comprise the key black spaces of community mental health care. There was a growth in advocacy work offering legal representation in mental health tribunals and coaching patients in the language of 'compliance' as a method of negotiating a way out of the system.[11] There was an expansion of monitoring, research and more general advocacy work by the Commission for Racial Equality and the Kings Fund which, from the standpoint of their own priorities, placed the mental health care system under critical scrutiny. In East London, and other areas too, the mental health pressure group MIND has taken an active interest in local black mental health issues throwing its support behind local specialized borough provision for black users. A common pattern is for local boroughs in concert with Social Services to provide black space within existing facilities.

The racialization of the community system as a response to the political pressure generated in the 1980s occurs in two ways. Either a black space is inserted into an existing facility so that an African-Caribbean or Somalian Women's users group is added-on to an otherwise unconsciously racialized, white space: or an existing facility is appropriated on behalf of black-users only. Black space also varies in the extent to which it is publicly announced with door signs and statements of commitment. There are hostels and half-way houses which have made a public commitment to be accessible to black-users. There are black advocacy projects operating around local hospitals and outreach projects which operate as a bridge between hospital and community. There are volunteer and support systems with an explicit public black focus. All of these facilities replicate, replace and manage the existing mental health care system rather than challenge its therapeutic strategies. There are fewer spaces offering alternate therapies such as the 'African-centred' holistic approaches offered at the African Caribbean Mental Health Association and the other centres which work with racism as a contributing factor to mental distress. A key element in racializing community mental health care is thus the appropriation of existing facilities on behalf of black users, rather than their reform. This means that generally the therapeutic strategies of the system remain the same.

STAFFING

Black staff play an important part in this appropriation and symbolic marking-out of space. The political commitment of centre staff to anti-racist initiatives - many see themselves as agents for political and social reform - and the implicit messages of welcome their presence offers to black-users were central features in racializing community provision. Only one centre which saw itself as a black space had an all white staff; what made it black was its commitment to working with black people. Staff conceptions of blackness and anti-racism varied a great deal. Some were content to provide a space in which black people could spend the day: and blackness in this context was a zone of occupation for black bodies. Others were more interested in reforming, training and managing their users' sense of blackness. In one centre the organizer was in despair over the users' decision to see *Jurassic Park* on their trip to the cinema instead of *Malcolm X*. Different versions of blackness led to disputes between workers in the same or adjacent and co-operating centres. Workers were acutely aware of the difficulties posed by the ways in which blackness was inserted into the existing system of provision: they were being asked to run black ghettoes in a highly problematic and cash-starved system. Many were immobilized by the simultaneous political pressure for ghettoization, and by the accusation of segregation. The racialization of community mental health worked by providing likeness between users and workers: it was the bodies and the political commitment of workers which defined a space as black; a heavily over-invested position to be placed in and one which took its toll in terms of job-related stress and burn-out rates.

SYMBOLS OF COLLECTIVE IDENTITY

The symbolic field of contextually organized social meanings making up blackness in centres was about forging a collective identity as a mechanism for counter assertion. Blackness was symbolized in centre iconography, in activities and in the management of the identities of its users. The iconography was that of a black diaspora: some centres had names invoking ancient black Egyptian civilizations, portraits of African-American civil rights leaders and African-Caribbean food; creating a comfort zone in which Nigerians, Asians and the elderly were consigned to the internal spaces and the vacant armchairs of the periphery. In centres which offered more than hanging-out space for black bodies, activities blackened and managed internal space giving expression to a certain range of black identities. In one centre the music club, a prestigious, male, activity aimed at allowing those with some musical talent to pay homage to black music with vocals, guitars and other instruments, was about marking internal black space.

Users in some centres were seen as students of identity: black bodies to be molded around the symbols of the diaspora. One centre leader, complaining at the assimilatedness of black East Enders in comparison to the more independent South Londoners, offered identity workshops dealing with 'empowerment', 'knowing who we are' and building 'positive images and role models'. Blackness in this way became a matter of training in the appropriate narratives of collective identity building. In dealing with us as researchers, some centres would wheel out their star students for interviews. Users, preferably male and under 40, with the right kind of story to tell - about the system's lack of understanding and brutality, and who *seem* all right and might possibly have been wrongly diagnosed - were prized territory.[12] Jennifer, who had the most highly worked narrative of all, we learned had already been interviewed by other research teams and did tours giving talks. Blackness, as the administrative invention of the community system, is a highly managed adjunct to anti-racist critique; with experiences, life stories and bodies being levered into the dominant narratives strands of protest.

MAKING THE BEST OF IT

Some users collude with centres' conceptions of blackness, others are excluded by it, or exempt themselves by asserting other versions of blackness and madness. Users, we found, decide which centres to use and how to use them. One of our informants, equipped with a bus pass, toured the facilities of East and North London and made discriminating use of what was available. Jon uses centres to run his own small business washing staff cars and supplying drugs; making sure he's around when the unemployment cheques arrive. Many use centres as an alternative to a life of isolation at home or on the streets as Jane suggests:

> I've got a lot out of this place - it's given me somewhere I belong - I've been pushed around from pillar to post for so long - It's just a sense of belonging somewhere and feeling welcome, where you're not scrutinised all the time and feel you're being watched. Nobody forces you to do anything and in a lot of places they introduce you and force you to take part in a lot of things or they sling you out...It's a godsend but I can't always rely on places like this - I've got to lead a normal life eventually which I'm not doing at the moment.

Centres may have their own conceptions of users, but users negotiate with these conceptions in pursuing their own projects within the limited scope of the available resources.

Conclusions

Although the lives of our informants were powerfully organised by the power/knowledge system of formal psychiatry and its outreach into the community, it is clear from their conceptions of schizophrenia, hospitalisation, drugs, centres, themselves and their own lives that these are 'poets of their own affairs' who make decisions about how to deal with symbolism and knowledge about them construed by others (de Certeau 1988:32-34). It would not, therefore, be entirely correct to characterise black schizophrenics as the racialized objects of the social regulatory mechanisms of psychiatry, as psychiatry's critics have claimed. Forced to negotiate with administrative conceptions of who they are, generated in the racialized spaces of both psychiatry and the community system which grew up to defend them from psychiatry, users of the system assert, in practice, their own versions of the community of community mental health services in East London. They generate their own conceptions of place with all of its symbolism, meaning, territory and social relationships with which they confront collective, administrative and cultural, notions of place. The administratively construed social relations of community psychiatry are much the same in other places, but what makes East London distinctive is the outcome of a dialogue between the administrative, the cultural and the existential. Much of what has been described in this paper - the race politics and the character of anti-racist action, forms of racialization and demographics of the area, the autobiographies of users, the peculiar landscape of local facilities and the character of its psychiatric wards and their staff - are specific to East London. Other things - the practice and social relationships of psychiatry, the problems posed by delivering services which are sensitive to various dimensions of ethnic and cultural difference, the narrative structure of the stories of schizophrenics themselves, and the need to provide for the chronically mentally distressed outside of institutional settings, are not special features of the East End, but are found in other parts of London, Britain and even in Quebec, where they take on the local configurations of place.

This article has shown that the racialization of space in community mental health has generated administrative versions of blackness and schizophrenia which counter those of psychiatry. This is an important form of counter assertion which has made facilities more user-friendly for those whose versions of themselves fit within the parameters of *centre blackness,* and is a welcomed departure from the unconscious and unchallenged white domination of mental health spaces. But black community facilities are limited both by their restricted sense of their users' identities, and by their position within the existing, and highly problematic, system of community psychiatric provision. The stories we heard point to some fundamental problems in the social relationships of psychiatry, its therapeutic strategies, and its understanding of human distress. The need, which most users voiced, for stability, belonging, jobs, housing: in short, forms of citizenship, is actively sabotaged by the ways in which the community system operates to create nomadic lives. The racialization of community space has secured improvements, but these are limited by the organisation of the system itself, which works against the needs of its users. More fundamental and racially articulate reforms are necessary to address the lived experience of those who are forced to use this system.

NOTES

1. I should like to thank Ian Toon for help with interviewing and for his insights without which this paper could not have been developed. I also acknowledge the financial assistance of the Social Science and Humanities Research Council of Canada and Concordia University, Montreal. Many thanks also to the centres cooperating with our research and to those users who shared their stories with us.

2. Racialization is a term used in the work of Robert Miles and refers to the ways in which issues and events acquire the symbolism of race.

3. 'Black' in this context refers to the terms in which African-Caribbeans were targeted by studies indicating prevalence rates for schizophrenia which were well above rates for the population as a whole (Knowles 1991), to the anti-racist defence mounted by and on behalf of this population and to the high proportion of non-whites living in the area of East London (Rix 1996:27).

4. This paper is based on a study which involved collecting life story narratives from black (Asians, Africans and African-Caribbean) people diagnosed as 'schizophrenic' in East, North and South London, as well as in Montreal. The use of the term 'black' is not intended to contest fragmentation and the racial politics of identity, it is rather one of the key terms in which the racialization of psychiatry and the struggles against it are cast.

5. Interviewers often had to acknowledge wellness of the interviewee before the interview could progress. Interviews, though mostly private, were often a *performance* of something and had a meaning for the informant.

6. Existential narratives are not purely stories of the self but are most likely worked-up with through interviews with psychiatrists, so that the patient's version of the

story contains elements of psychiatric explanation. In this sense existential narratives have a strong administrative element, but are controlled by the storyteller.

7. Demonstrating the authenticity of the 'illness' was often as issue in the stories we heard and implies that mental illness could be faked.

8. I should like to thank Patrick Knowles for this point and for various other insights on how community mental health works on a more practical basis.

9. Centres refers to hostels, half-way houses, projects and day centres. In the course of the research project on which this is based we investigated some of each of this kind of facility.

10. All of our informants were 'distressed' and needed help and resources in order to organise their lives in ways which took account of that distress. The central issue is not the veracity of their schizophrenia but the ways in which they understand and live with it and whether there are forms of therapeutic or social provision which make this task more or less difficult.

11. For example the African Caribbean Mental Health Association, Brixton.

12. This contrasts sharply with the priorities of Mental Health Trusts for which the chronically mentally ill carry a high price tag in the machinations of the internal market. This raises the issue of administrative belonging with highly mobile people being tracked so that fees can be collected from the trust area 'owning' the patient.

REFERENCES

Barham, P., *Schizophrenia and Human Values*, Blackwell, Oxford 1984.

Bloch, A., 'Refugees in Newham', Tim Butler and Michael Rustin (eds), *Rising in the East: the Regeneration of East London?*, Lawrence and Wishart, London 1996.

Cohen, P., 'Homing Devices', V. Amit-Talai and C. Knowles (eds), *Resituating Identities: The Politics of Race, Ethnicity and Culture*, Broadview Press, Peterborough 1996.

Cohen, P., 'All White on the Night? Narratives of Nativism on the Isle of Dogs', T. Butler and M. Rustin (eds), *Rising in the East: the Regeneration of East London?*, Lawrence and Wishart, London 1996, pp170-196.

de Certeau, M., *The Practice of Everyday Life*, The University of Los Angeles Press, Berkeley 1988.

Francis, E., 'Black People "Dangerousness" and Psychiatric Compulsion', A. Bracx and C. Grimshaw (eds), *Mental Health Care in Crisis*, Pluto, London 1989.

Freeman, M., *Rewriting the Self: History, Memory, Narrative*, Routledge, London 1993.

Hackney Schizophrenia Guide, London 1993.

Keith, M. and Pile, S., 'Introduction Part 1: The Politics of Place', M. Keith and S. Pile (eds), *Place and the Politics of Identity*, Routledge, London 1993, pp1-21.

Knowles, C., 'Afro-Caribbeans and Schizophrenia: How Does Psychiatry Deal With Issues of Race, Culture and Ethnicity?' *Journal of Social Policy*, Number 20, Volume 2, pp173-90.

Littlewood, R. and Lipsedge, M., 'Psychiatric Illness Among British Afro-Caribbean's', *British Medical Journal*, Number 296, Volume 2, pp950-1.

Littlewood, R., 'Ideology, Camouflage or Contingency? Racism in British Psychiatry', *Transcultural Psychiatric Research Review* XXX,3 pp.83-92

Rix, Vikki (1996) Social and Demographic Change in East London Tim Butler and Michael Rustin (eds). *Rising in the East: the Regeneration of East London?*, Lawrence and Wishart, London 1996, pp20-60.

Sashidharan, S.P., 'Epidemiology, Ethnicity and Schizophrenia', W. Ahmed (ed), *Race and Health in Contemporary Britain*, Open University Press, Milton Keynes 1992.

Winant, H., 'Racial Formation and Hegemony: Global and Local Developments', A. Rattansi and S. Westwood (eds), *Racism, Modernity and Identity on the Western Front*, Polity, Cambridge 1994, pp.266-290.

Three Case Studies

Young People, Family Life and Education in Barking and Dagenham

Margaret O'Brien and Deborah Jones

> Margaret O'Brien and Deborah Jones report on a study conducted in one of the localities investigated by Peter Willmott in the 1950s - Barking and Dagenham - but from the vantage point of young people in the 1990s. The study consisted of a questionnaire survey of 600 young people's views about contemporary family life and kinship patterns and follow-up interviews with a sub-sample of the young people, their parents and a grandparent. The study has examined the transmission of family cultures between generations, and explored place as a context for identity construction and educational underachievement in a relatively stable, predominantly white working class locality.

FROM THE 1950s researchers and policy-makers, notably Peter Willmott and Michael Young, have carefully examined the state of family life in inner and outer East London. In this paper we present some impressions which are emerging from a study of family life in an Outer East London borough in the 1990s. We have revisited one of the localities investigated by Peter Willmott in the 1950s - Barking and Dagenham - but from the vantage point of the 1990s with all its particular preoccupations, some of which are not too far from those of the 1950s. It should be remembered that Willmott and Young discovered the family by accident: the original focus of the project behind 'Family and Kinship in East London' was housing and the impact of moving from the inner city to an outer housing estate. In the 1957 introduction to their book they remark:

We were surprised to discover that the wider family, far from having disappeared, was still very much alive in the middle of London. This finding seemed to us of more interest than anything we had been led to expect...[so] We decided, although we hit on it more or less accidentally, to make our main subject the wider family (p12).

A major backdrop to our investigation has been the intense debate through the 1980s and into the 1990s about the decline in what have been called family values: on the political right expressed as a concern about the decline in marriage rates, the increase in divorce and about a too easy acceptance of non-traditional ways of living; on the political left and centre expressed more in terms of worry about apparent lack of commitment and support between the generations or between men and women. What both ends of the political spectrum have in common is a concern about the impact of familial, economic and cultural change on children (Brannen and O'Brien, 1996).

When the Barking and Dagenham study was originally devised it was conceived of as a mapping of family and kinship patterns in an urban community initially from the perspectives of children and then working backwards through the generations to examine the transmission of family cultures between generations. We were interested in children's constructions of contemporary family life - their views on 'the family' and on their own daily experiences - at home, at school, at work and at leisure. Were these young people questioning traditional values such as a belief in the importance of marriage, children within marriage, the value of kin, self-sacrifice as for instance, the individualization thesis might predict? (Beck, 1992). The importance of place as a context for identity construction and agency in social relations has been somewhat overlooked by general theories of global change such as Becks'. We have used the specificity of Barking and Dagenham, a homogeneous and relatively stable urban community, to aid our understanding of contemporary family life and how the historical formation of a place impacts upon identity construction. As Doreen Massey (1984) reminds us,

> 'General processes' *never* work themselves out in pure form. There is always specific circumstances, a particular history, a particular place or location. What is at issue - and to put it in geographical terms - is the articulation of the general with the local (the particular) to produce qualitatively different outcomes in different localities (p9).

At the outset of the study we were not aware of just how specific were the contours and dynamics of Barking and Dagenham and as the study has progressed the issue of educational underachievement in the borough and the links between family cultures, social mobility and educational pathways have taken a central focus.

The study began with a survey of the childhood generation in 1994, which also included a daily diary which respondents completed for one week. We recruited a sample of 600 young people, drawn from class groups in six of the eight state schools in Barking and Dagenham (there are no private secondary schools in the borough). After piloting we opted for children in the anticipatory stages of the first significant national examinations - average age 14 years in order to examine daily life at a transitional period - on the margins of adulthood and childhood. Two years later respondents were followed up for individual inter-generational household interviews with the target child, the parents and a grandparent.

In this article we shall examine the historical development of Barking and Dagenham to aid our understanding of the socio-demographic and cultural characteristics of the borough in the 1990s. A central theme is the power of the past and the power of the local in shaping the culture of a place and its people. In particular we shall focus on how the area has remained relatively immune to global economic change, at least in so far as this is related to male employment patterns and patterns of family life. The community of Barking and Dagenham has been relatively successful to date in coping with economic change. However there is local concern that the youth of Barking and Dagenham are not capitalizing on the educational opportunities available to them, repeating the educational patterns of the parental generation. We shall illustrate some of these themes using three case studies of contemporary families living in the locality.

Barking and Dagenham: 1950s

During the interwar period, the London County Council built thirteen 'cottage estates' outside London to rehouse people living in inner city slums. The Becontree Council Estate in Dagenham was one of those thirteen over-spill estates. People moved from extremely close-knit, impoverished but nevertheless stable and supportive working-class communities in East London to recreate a new community in the suburbs. Although conditions in the slums were extremely overcrowded, with poor sanitation and unhealthy accommodation, oral history sources, (in particular Rubinstein, Andrews and Schweitzer, 1991) reveal that these close-knit communities were a source of strength for many people living in poverty. This was a time of great uncertainty, when the 1930s recession was beginning and jobs were scarce. To uproot from a supportive community for one in the country with a poorly developed infrastructure, an absence of educational and medical resources involved a great deal of risk for many people. However, it was also a challenge and for many families it brought, at the very least, potential for new opportunities and experiences.

Willmott's 1950s study *The Evolution of a Community* (1963), showed how the cockney, mainly white, East End families, highly organized by kin, often relocated together or sometimes the younger generation would migrate first, soon to be followed by their parents. As children of the first generation to migrate, grew up and married themselves, families still remained geographically close to one another. By the late 1950s Peter Willmott found that four-fifths of married couples who grew up on the estate and whose parents were still alive had them living close by. Traditional family forms prevailed: 78 per cent of Willmott's sample were married, less than 1 per cent divorced and 13 per cent single.

Dagenham of the 1950s had a high level of spatial uniformity, described by Willmott at the time as an area of vast flatness, openness and uniformity, with a 'monotone air', lacking in visual contrast. This was matched by a socially uniform culture. Overwhelmingly working-class in character, Willmott described Dagenham as a 'one class colony'. His sample consisted of 89 per cent employed in skilled manual, semi-skilled manual and unskilled manual occupations. Only 4 per cent were employed in professional and managerial occupations. One-fifth of all men and 6 per cent of all employed women on the estate were employed in Fords motor works and its associated industries. Educational achievements and parental expectations were low. Indeed, Willmott quotes a national study carried out in the 1950s by Moser and Scott who found that Barking and Dagenham had the third highest proportion of children leaving school under the age of fifteen (84 per cent) and the lowest proportion of young people between fifteen and twenty-four in full-time education.

Barking & Dagenham - The 1990s

The 1991 Census indicates that on the whole the population is stable and is still predominantly white and working-class in character. The borough is, however, experiencing some of the national changes which are occurring across the UK, Europe and other westernized countries. For example, one is beginning to see a pluralization of family forms within Barking and Dagenham, reflected, for instance, by an increase in lone parent households and dual-worker households. The proportion of births outside marriage have increased. In 1991 over one third, (36.5 per cent) of births occurred outside marriage, which is higher than the national average of 31 per cent. The borough also has high fertility rates, especially for young people. Barking and Dagenham has the second highest rate of teenage births in and outside of marriage when compared to other inner and outer East London boroughs (Annual Abstracts of Greater London Statistics, 1992).

Whilst the locality has not been immune to industrial decline, Rix's (1996) analysis of the 1991 Census and social change in East London, points out that Barking and Dagenham has been more successful at coping with the consequences of economic restructuring than any other East London borough. Despite the fact that the locality has experienced a decline in manufacturing, Barking and Dagenham has the highest economic activity rates for men, the lowest proportion of economically inactive men, (27.3 per cent) and the highest proportion of men in full-time employment, (50.4 per cent) compared with the rest of East London.[1] This is perhaps surprising in an area with the lowest percentage of people in London with a degree, higher degree or diploma (Barking and Dagenham Borough Profile, 1993).

There is still educational underachievement in the community. In 1991 only 3.5 per cent of those over eighteen years had a degree or diploma, compared to 3.6 per cent in 1981 (1991 Census). In fact, Barking and Dagenham has the lowest proportion of people with such qualifications in London, the London-wide average being 18.5 per cent (1991 Census). Historically, there has also been long-standing pupil underachievement in the borough which has been at or near the bottom of the DFE league table for some time. Over the last decade, the strategic aim of the borough has been to achieve national averages on all educational indicators by the turn of the century. (London Borough of Barking and Dagenham, Education Department).[2] There have been some improvements, but progress is slow and checkered with much variation between individual schools. On the key indicator of 5 or more high grade GCSE passes (A-C), the borough has seen improvements from 16 per cent in 1992 to 20 per cent in 1993 and 28 per cent in 1994. However, 1995 revealed a slowing down of the rate of improvement at this level, with again 28 per cent achieving high grades, well below the national average of 48 per cent. Sustained improvement, at the level seen in previous years is required if the borough is to meet national targets by the end of the decade.

Our original survey highlights some inconsistencies between what young people in Barking and Dagenham anticipate for their future in terms of further education and careers and behavioural patterns as reflected in recent educational statistics. Although a significant majority expressed a wish to continue in further education post sixteen years, in reality this is not happening. Barking and Dagenham has the lowest percentage of young people in education post sixteen years, compared to all other London boroughs (this was identified as a problem by Moser & Scott in the 1950s). In fact, there has been a decline in the percentage staying on post-sixteen since the last figures were published for 1994. In 1995, 58.5 per cent of young people remained in further education post-sixteen, compared with 9 in 10 sixteen year olds in the UK as a whole (*School Leaver Destinations*, 1996 & *Social Trends* 1996) .

Kinship, family life and education

We were interested in whether the sample of young people of Barking and Dagenham in the 1990s were surrounded by relatives, in much the same manner as Willmott described in *The Evolution of A Community*. Although Willmott notes some variations in the community, he concluded that: 'In part, Dagenham is the East End reborn', particularly for those families that had grown up in the area. 'In all sorts of ways relationships with kin follow familiar patterns. Women see their mothers, and their fathers, more than men do...The mother's home, again, is the most common centre for her daughters.' His vantage point was an adult sample of married couples, whereas we were looking at kinship through the accounts of fourteen year olds, the majority of whom had lived in the area since birth.

THE SALIENCE OF KIN

Like Willmott our findings show that there is still a pattern of 'matrilocality', with 47 per cent of the sample having their maternal grandparents living in Barking and Dagenham, compared with 38 per cent of paternal grandparents (these proportions include co-residential grandparents). This proximity is similar to that found by Willmott in 1959: 44 per cent of grandparents co-resided or lived locally (see Table 1). Fewer grandparents co-resided when compared to Willmott's sample (2 per cent vs 17 per cent), however a further 2 per cent of contemporary households contained great grandparents.

The central focus of the maternal line for emotional and material support is reflected in the following quote from a woman in her forties,

Table 1. Proximity of Kin (%)		
	Dagenham 1959	Barking & Dagenham 1994*
Same dwelling	17	10
Local	27	51
Further away	65	49

Source: Dagenham (1959), Willmott (1963) p 25.
Willmott's data on co-resident parents only.
* The data in this column does not total 100 per cent as data derived from two questions (coresidence and proximity of non-coresident kin). Barking and Dagenham Study.

married and with three boys of her own :

> I mean my mum and I have a wonderful relationship. I mean we're never apart from when we've been abroad, not last year but the year before. I mean last year we went away with me mum and dad, well we've not even ever been on holiday without them. ... My mum and dad em, they've helped us all the way through.

Later she explains :

> Because I think you'll find as you do these interviews the daughter's mother is more in the family unit than the father's mother. They seem to be more close.

Table 2 shows the frequency of contact with paternal and maternal grandparents. Overall, contact with maternal grandparents is highest: 35 per cent see her weekly, 16 per cent daily and 49 per cent occasionally. In general frequency of contact with paternal grandparents is less than half that of maternal grandparental contact.

The maternal grandmother was also the most popular grandparent.

Table 2. Contact with Grandparents (%)				
	Maternal		Paternal	
	GdM N=412	GdF N=292	GdM N=370	GdF N=254
Daily	16	13	7	6
Weekly	35	31	24	18
Occasional	49	56	69	76

She is talked to more frequently by grand-children and the most frequently mentioned topic of conversation is school and educational matters 'how I'm getting on at school' 44 per cent of the sample cited this, followed by the topic of leisure (24 per cent).

Here, Richard Morris, aged seventeen, describes his main daily activity with his previously co-resident maternal grandmother: 'She'd normally be in when I came home from school so it would be like, "How's school, did you enjoy it, what did you do?"'.

As well as grandparents, we also looked at contact with wider kin in the neighbourhood: Seventy-two per cent of the sample had a relative visit their home within the last week, 15 per cent a month ago, and only 10 per cent not for a long time. Whilst half of the sample reported having no kin living in their neighbourhood, of the remainder a significant minority had five or more relatives living close by (see table 3). Indeed 20 per cent with nearby kin had a network of over ten relatives living locally.

Table 3. Numbers of Kin in Neighbourhood (%)	
1-4 relatives	63
5-9 relatives	21
10-19 relatives	11
20-29 relatives	4
30 + relatives	5
(N=276, excluding those with no kin in neighbourhood (N= 271) and missing value cases)	

Daily and weekly contact with maternal grandmother was most frequent for those children having five or more kin living locally. These kin relationships need further exploration but the pattern is suggestive of an extended family network with a high level of interdependence and cohesiveness for a significant minority of Barking and Dagenham families. The Morris family, one of the cases we will be discussing below exemplifies this family network:

Mrs Morris is married with three children; our target child Richard is the middle son. In addition to her parents and in-laws, she has two married brothers living in the locality. Her husband's married sister and their two children also live nearby. Mrs Morris explains:

Any other relatives living in the area ?

I've got a sister-in law and my other sister-in-law. Both my husband's sisters live in the area. Both my brothers live in the area. My mother-in-law and father-in-law live just up the road.

There is regular contact with kin on both sides of the family. Aunts, uncles, cousins and grandparents often meet up at each others houses. They also participate in day-trips, holidays and family parties together. As Mrs Morris explains:

> It doesn't matter if it's not very far it's just that we all get out together ... we went to Canvey on Monday ... Jamie (youngest son) come and my sister-in law who is, if you can imagine like she's my sister-in-law but she's my best friend ... it's like two family units in one. Because we're so close we go on holiday to Butlin's and they're here all the time. I mean when Pam (husband's sister) and her John had their dodgy times they came here to live - Pam and the two youngest children, and John had the two eldest boys over their home.

THE MORRIS HOUSEHOLD - 'THE WORKING CLASS SURVIVORS'

The Morris household represents a family culture that is highly cohesive and relatively stable. We have called this family 'the working-class survivors' because, in spite of a lack of parental qualifications and a general disregard for formal education, there has been no unemployment within the three generations surveyed. In this family there is continuity of tradition across the three generations surveyed and for the time being at least, it is highly supportive and protective against change. This familial culture resonates with the work of Paul Thompson, (1993) whose argument that strong family cultures, tend not to promote upward mobility, but instead are normally 'conservative and protective'.

The Morris family have a large network of extended kin. Both sets of grandparents moved to the borough when they themselves were children. There is regular contact and support from both the maternal and paternal grandparents. However, the maternal line for contact and informal support is more apparent. Until quite recently the maternal grandparents actually lived with their daughter, Barbara. Here the maternal grandmother describes the special bond between mothers and their daughters, an inter-generational behavioural pattern:

> You are closer to your daughter aren't you? You can't help it. I mean my boys have been very good since I lost my husband... but their children are still not close like Barbara's (daughter) boys... I mean it was the same with me I suppose. I mean my mum and dad idolized mine, especially Barbara, because she was their only grandaughter.

The maternal grandparents, Mr and Mrs Cottle, moved to Dagenham from Canning Town when they were young. They were both locally educated. Mr Cottle, a coaler has recently died from an industrial disease. Mrs Cottle, sees her daughter and grandchildren every day. She explains how she sees her role as a grandmother: 'I looked after them as babies, but then all her kids are half mine anyway ... they're more like me own. So I think, they're just as much my children as hers'.

The paternal grandparents, Mr and Mrs Morris (Senior) originate from The Isle of Dogs and West Ham, and moved to Dagenham during the war after they were bombed out. Mrs Morris was 15 years old when she came to live in Dagenham from the East End. Both had an intermittent education and were married at 21 years after a long courtship. They went on to have three children. Mr and Mrs Morris (Senior) have adopted a non-interventionist approach in relation to child-rearing. She firmly believes that although parents may have ambitions for their children, they have to respect their children's right to follow their own instincts in life. However, discipline and guidance within the private sphere of the home is described in a more structured way and there are certain codes of practice centred around respect, which must be observed. For example, Mrs Morris explains: 'You're your own person, but providing you've got respect for your mum and dad and nans, and the family then everything is fine'.

However, outside the home, in the public sphere, codes of practice allow for more autonomy. For example, in relation to her eldest daughter, Mrs Morris explains:

> They (teachers) came over from the school and begged us to tell her to go to college. I wouldn't beg any of mine. I said to her, 'what is it that you want to do with your life ?' She said , 'I want to get a job and get on', and I said 'fine', She said 'I want money in me pocket' and I said, 'Well, you do whatever you want to do, providing it's respectful'. I wanted her to go, but in the end it's up to the individual, you can't make them do it.

Richard Morris, 17 yrs, is our target child. He is now at college studying for a Btec in a vocational subject. He has already had two well-paid job offers. Richard has recently become engaged and plans to marry his fiancée as soon as he is established in a secure job. Outside of the family, he has few friends. In fact, his social life centres around the immediate and extended family. In particular, he has a close relationship with his parents and his grandparents. His grandmother explains:

> He's a loner, he doesn't need friends ... I said to Barbara (daughter), yesterday, about his party because he's 18 this year and she's having a

party for him and she said 'Well, Richard hasn't got any friends'. So I turned round and said, 'Well he must get some' and she says 'No. What does he need friends for, is what he said, when they only let you down. Family don't'. Apparently he did have one good friend Terry ... and he let him down.

Richard's profound sense of attachment to his family and wider kin has served to dilute his academic potential. Indeed, Richard was advised by the school to enter the sixth form and register for 'A' levels. His decision to leave school at sixteen and enrol on a vocational course resonated with his familial culture, a way of life which is firmly embedded in work as opposed to academic tradition. Richard's parents and grandparents are sceptical of the need for formal qualifications. Mr Morris left school at fourteen with no qualifications. He gives a rich description of his employment history. There has been no experience of unemployment in either family. I asked Mr Morris for his views on education:

Do you think formal qualifications are important ?

No. There's a lot of people who've got qualifications.... I mean, like my boys stayed on and that, but they're still fighting, they're still fighting to get jobs. I mean alright he's got a part-time job in Sainsbury's for a few bob, but that's not what they've worked for.

So you feel differently because of your son's experience or have you always felt like that ?

Well I think they're (qualifications) not important because I came out (of school) when I was a kid. I didn't have nothing, I could have the pick of any job I wanted. They'd take me on, do anything, do any apprenticeship, anything I wanted. I went and worked as a toolmaker, I didn't enjoy that. I went as an apprentice mechanic for three years and because it was so low paid and that, I left that, got fed up. I went to Fords, took a couple of exams in there and became an inspector. I left there and went into ship cargoes, worked in there, didn't like it, so I went back to Fords. I left Fords, went to college and took up a trade (bricklaying) and you can see I do all this (pointing to his house). So to me, school didn't really give me what I wanted.

And do you still feel that applies today ?

Yes, because the kids are coming out and there isn't no work for them. I brought my kids up that you've got to find jobs. All my boys, from as soon as they can, have had paper rounds. I say, at least you can turn 'round and say to them (employers) look I have tried, I've been out, I've had a paper round all my life. They have gone out and tried to do something. I think they should be at work ... because, well the way I look at it, the longer they're waiting the harder it is to get a job. If there were plenty of jobs they could stay at college as long as they want. But, it's getting harder and harder to find jobs. I think they should try and find a job and do work and then get the experience and do their college work at the same time. I think that the governors should let them go to college in the evenings. Then they've got time to work and get the experience and do their college work at the same time. Otherwise, when they finish (their studies), they say to them "have you got any experience?" What do you turn 'round and say .... "Well no, I've been at college for the last three years".

Taylor, Evans and Fraser (1996) in *A Tale of Two Cities*, consider the post-industrial experience of two northern cities, namely Sheffield and Manchester. Their research suggests that local cultural difference shaped by the specific historical legacy of a place, have resulted in two quite distinctive experiences of regeneration. Up until the 1970s Sheffield had experienced relatively full employment, giving the impression locally of being impervious to international competition. The local 'structure of feeling' was that hard work or 'grafting' would see them through. Manchester on the other hand, has been more enthusiastically involved in economic regeneration. It was the first industrial city in England and as such is perhaps more accustomed to being at the cutting edge of change. The theoretical underpinning of their analysis stresses: '... the way in which a local structure of feeling, understood as a mediation of the local labour market, in the historical past and in contemporary experience, might help generate a sense of resistance or adaptation to global economic transformation' (p14).

In this same way, the particular characteristics of Barking and Dagenham's local population combined with local labour market opportunities may have exerted a particular influence on social attitudes towards education. Barking and Dagenham has never been dependent on one major industry in the same way that many northern towns have been. This may explain why the borough has adapted more successfully than other East London boroughs to industrial restructuring. Relatively low levels of male unemployment may be explained by an inter-generational tendency within the local culture, characterized by resilience and adaptability in the face of economic change and uncertainty. Indeed, in the above quote Mr Morris illustrates the rich diversity of local employment opportunities available to working-class men of Barking and Dagenham throughout the post-war period. He has survived by 'getting by' and 'making do' without formal qualifications. The borough is also geographically well-placed being as it is on the border of the more prosperous county of Essex; no doubt an important consumer market for the self-employed especially during the 1980s economic boom and very much so still in the 1990s.

The 'local structure of feeling' evident within this family is embedded in work or 'hard graft', rather than education. As Mr Morris explains: '... I mean I've had to really graft to get what we've got. I want them to graft but I don't want them to have to do what work I've had, like in the pouring rain, snow and everything'.

This extended family provide a secure, protective environment from a world of uncertainty and change. In fact as a family group they have been relatively successful to date - there have been no divorces, unemployment or significant family conflicts within either the parental or grandparental generations. Mr Morris's description of his employment history is indicative of a hard-working, resilient and adaptable man. His son likewise has been successful in spite of his low GCSE passes. It is unclear, however, whether a lack of educational resources will allow the next generation to compete successfully in a less certain world. However, where family norms and expectations are perceived to have worked well for two generations, they may well be adopted by the younger generation.

THE NEWMAN HOUSEHOLD - 'THE OUTSIDERS'

In the second case study, we introduce the Newman household as a way of illustrating the power of place and stability and how these impact upon family life. In particular, this case study highlights how a socially homogenous place such as Barking and Dagenham creates difficulties for individuals whose behavioural patterns conflict with cultural norms, 'the outsiders within'. In the following case study we show how incoming residents who exhibit different and more diverse ways of living are feared. We go on to explore how the power of place creates buffers against innovation which protect against change within family life.

The Newman household give a rich description of Barking and Dagenham from an outsiders' perspective. This family culture is 'New Age' and consists of mum, step-dad, and three children. The eldest daughter is now fifteen years old and is taking her GCSEs this summer. She plans to study media & communication studies at college, and eventually hopes to go on to university. Kate, her mother, is forty-two years old and was born in a relatively prosperous part of Essex. She experienced a middle-class upbringing and describes herself as having been raised with a knowledge of opera and ballet ... 'a high-church upbringing'.

Kate left school at eighteen with six 'O' levels and one 'A' level. She has now returned to college and hopes eventually to take up a career in teaching. Kate's relationship with her mother was fraught with difficulties and conflict, a woman she found too restricting and narrow-minded. Kate now has infrequent contact with her. At the age of twenty-two she married a man (Tom) she met at work, and went to live with him in Dagenham, 'to escape the situation at home'. He was a Dagenham man, with a large network of extended kin living in the borough. His grandparents were of the first generation to migrate from Bow (inner East London) when the estate was first built in the 1930s.

Kate and Tom had three children together but it soon became apparent that they were ill-matched and Kate developed a social life separate from her husband. Eventually, after coping with a series of his affairs, she left him. Kate has now remarried a man from outside of the area. Together they continue to live as outsiders in the borough; their visual difference and individuality the cause of many problems for them and the children.

Kate describes what it was like moving into the borough as a recently married woman in her early twenties. She describes her feelings about living as an outsider in a highly cohesive community:

How does it feel living in this borough ?

Very strange. I've tried very hard to fit in. I was going crazy when I gave up work, ... considered eating the wallpaper ! Anyway, I went to a mother and toddler group, but no one would speak to me because of my posh accent. It was a kind of inverted snobbery. What broke the ice one day was when a boy came in delivering the mail and he had a beautiful bottom and I pretended to grab it, One of the girls saw it and she said 'ere you're one of us, you aren't posh are you !'... and that was that, we became good friends.

Have you ever thought about moving ?

I would love to. If people left us alone we would be fine.

The 'New Age' characteristics of the Newman family created difference, and an experience of being ostracized, particularly by youths in the area. On the day of the interview Kate was dressed in a long black dress, adorned with lots of jewellery. Her lip was pierced and her long hair dyed. In the living-room, art nouveau prints, Indian cushions and candles contributed to the hippy feel. A rota for housework duties was displayed on the mantle-piece along with numerous books and videos. The family have on several occasions been the victims of threatening behaviour, windows have been smashed, eggs thrown at the door and verbal abuse and name-calling have become a regular experience. Kate explains that the family now have a police patrol at night and went on to outline her views on why she feels this is necessary: 'It isn't just us, there's a Vietnamese family and someone else round the (place name) ... just one or two people who stand out I suppose. You're not allowed to stand out, you've got to be the same as everybody else'.

Cultural expectations in a cohesive and somewhat inward-looking community allow little room for individuals to challenge perceived norms. Kate goes on to describe the problems her first husband, a local man experienced in his youth whilst expressing an individual identity in conflict with expected norms: 'He wanted to wear long hair, but in order not to get beaten up, he had to wear skinhead clothes...... For him it was a question of survival because it's Dagenham and they tend to think with their fists'.

Likewise, Sarah her daughter feels isolated at school due to her visual difference and her somewhat aspirant expectations for the future. She explains: 'They think I'm a bit odd as I tend to dye my hair strange colours. They're (other girls at her school) all saps[3], they all want to grow up and have babies. It's Dagenham mentality, they don't know any better ... their parents have loads of children and that's what they're used to'.

Later, Kate describes her perception of families in Dagenham, from an outsider's point of view: 'There are a lot of families with a capital F 'round here ... Apparently when I divorced Tom, I divorced the whole family. I think it's ... from what I've seen, I think it's an East End thing, because it's ... because they're a very very loyal family, they took his side'.

Thompson (1993) has argued that in communities with strong kin ties social mobility is low and that the loosening of those ties may be an important precursor for upward social mobility. This model seems to partially explain the pattern of social homogeneity and low educational achievement in Barking and Dagenham since the 1950s at least for the white, working-class community. The Newman household live in the borough as outsiders. They do not have a network of extended kin living locally and most of their social life is conducted outside of the borough.

WHY FOCUS ON EDUCATION ?

The results of our original survey of 600 young people, display examples of both continuity and change. On the familial front, the young people of our initial sample have a clear idea about what they anticipate for their future. Often these expectations are centred around marriage, childbearing and family solidarity, but with a view to more equality between the sexes than in their parents' generation, and a companionate relationship (88 per cent envisaged getting married at about twenty-four and twenty-six was the average age for the start of childbearing). However, they also have high expectations for a career and further education, which exemplifies change. They are living between two worlds; the traditional model based around family obligations and commitment and the new model of self-fulfilment and individual enhancement.

The majority had occupational and educational aspirations way beyond their parents' experiences. For instance, 67 per cent of the sample had ambitions towards a professional/managerial job whilst only 23 per cent of fathers and 18 per cent of mothers currently worked in these occupations. Similarly, the vast majority, 80 per cent of the sample, wished to pursue some form of further education after year Eleven, mostly staying on to the sixth form or going to sixth form college or having some other form of education. Only 13 per cent were expecting to go to work at sixteen.

Moreover, an overwhelming majority of young people did not wish to pursue a career along the lines of their mother and father. Ninety-one per cent of the sample did not identify with their mother's job. Fifty-nine per cent of these felt that their mother's job was 'boring' or they had 'other ambitions'. Similarly, a majority (83 per cent) did not identify with their father's job, for the same main reason 'boring/other ambitions' (55 per cent).

However, although our study highlights change at least in the educational expectations of young people, there is still educational underachievement in the borough. It is the disparity between the aspirant educational and career expectations of the majority of young people in our original study and the reality as revealed by educational statistics which needs further exploration. We are exploring this dichotomy through intergenerational interviews.

THE BROWN HOUSEHOLD - 'BETWEEN TWO WORLDS'

This household illuminates the theme of living between two worlds. Jamie is a high achiever (9 grade A GCSEs) and has high career expectations whilst at the same time being family centred. At the time of the interview,

Jamie was revising for his 'A' levels having secured a provisional place at university to study English. However, at the age of eighteen he is also an expectant father, an apparently planned event. He has a strong sense of place and a local embeddedness, is fiercely loyal to Barking and Dagenham, and has no plans to move out of the borough.

Jamie's parents have no formal educational experience beyond the compulsory school leaving age. His mother left school at fifteen with no qualifications and his father regularly played truant from school. However, although they lack formal qualifications and experience themselves Mrs Brown, in particular, has a profound interest in her son's education. They may not be involved in the sense of helping with school work and homework but this family illustrate how change may be created through parental encouragement and interest alone. Such an association has been found in other research, for instance Tizard *et al*'s (1988) study of attainment amongst inner city primary schoolchildren found that a major factor in determining a child's success appeared to be parental interest and encouragement.

Jamie's parents moved to Dagenham from Islington fifty years ago when they themselves were young children. There were already relatives living in Becontree when they arrived. His paternal grandfather since deceased, was a railway worker and his grandmother was casually employed in factory work. Jamie's mother enjoyed school and generally had a positive school experience. At fifteen he found work in a local office. When she was seventeen she met her husband at a local fair and fell pregnant soon after. They were married at eighteen. Mrs Brown continued to work after the birth of her first son, a decision she now regrets feeling that it had an adverse effect on her firstborn. Twelve years later she gave birth to her second child (Jamie) and her third child was born a few years later. This time Mrs Brown gave up work to devote herself to full-time motherhood. This, she feels has benefited her second and third born.

Mr Brown is in his early fifties and is long-term unemployed. Unfortunately he would not be interviewed, explaining 'it's not my sort of thing really'. His wife mentioned that Mr Brown lacked confidence in talking about educational matters which appeared to be connected to his earlier life experience. She describes how he had a negative school experience. He frequently played truant from school, in order to assist his father who was a florist/street trader. His father is deceased and his octogenarian mother lives alone. There is frequent contact with the paternal grandmother, the last surviving grandparent who lives locally.

Jamie is engaged to his long-term girlfriend who is also studying 'A' levels, and is expecting a child at the end of the year. In this respect he is repeating the marital pattern of his parents. However with regard to education and employment, Jamie is looking for personal fulfilment and is highly ambitious in his expectations for the future.

Conclusion

An inter-generational tendency within the local culture characterized by resilience and adaptability in the face of social and economic change is part of the local 'structure of feeling' in Barking and Dagenham and may partially explain how the residents have adapted to economic change in the post-Fordist era. Our initial analysis of interviews is showing how some contemporary families of up to three generations, such as the Morris household, have successfully negotiated change in the economy, remaining in work, with few or no educational qualifications. Many individuals have succeeded through 'ducking and diving' (Hobbs, 1995), non-formal ways of 'getting by' and 'hard graft' . For men especially, 'hard graft' and earning money through informal contacts have been successful survival strategies. The strong local economy may also be able to support the growing numbers of young mothers found in the community.

Indeed, resilience, adaptability, determination and survival in the face of adversity have been well documented as a characteristic feature of East Londoners. Living with extreme poverty in the slum tenements of inner East London was described by social researchers such as Mayhew (1851) and Booth (1889) in the nineteenth century. A recent article in *The Guardian* (14/08/96) relating to community regeneration initiatives in Tower Hamlets, one of the most deprived boroughs in the UK, opens with the sentence 'For most people in the East End of London resilience remains a traditional prerequisite for survival'. Likewise, the early migrants to Barking and Dagenham having been uprooted from a close-knit community had to contend with a very different way of life in a place with poorly developed infrastructures, little local employment (apart from Fords), few pubs and physical isolation. Adaptability and resilience were necessary prerequisites for survival in 1930s Dagenham. Rubinstein, Andrews and Schweitzer (1991) recorded residents' recollections of the move to Dagenham from East London. Many of the recollections depict ambivalence about their new environment. Here one of the early migrants explains: 'I missed the East End when I first came here. I didn't have my mum to help me and it was a terrible wrench ... I wasn't happy but of course I had to get used to it'. Likewise another migrant reflects: '... I just couldn't tolerate Dagenham.

There was nothing here. Nice and open but I just couldn't stand it'.

The individualization thesis as outlined by Beck (1992) needs to take account of the importance of place and its associated historical and spatial legacies when attempting to capture the complexities of contemporary family life. As shown in this paper, the majority of our sample are not questioning traditional family values, 88 per cent expect to get married at about twenty-four and expect to raise a family of their own at twenty-six, whilst at the same time having high expectations for a career and personal fulfilment. However, educational statistics reveal that a significant number of young people are not taking full advantage of the educational opportunities available to them, repeating the patterns of their parental and grand parental generations. The percentage of young people in Barking and Dagenham gaining high grade GCSES continues to be well below the national average. In addition there is still a tendency for a significant minority to leave school at sixteen and teenage fertility rates are alarmingly high.

It is, of course, the case that, in relative terms, the young generation of Barking and Dagenham is becoming more educationally qualified than the generations before them. To date however it appears that strong, traditional family and cultural processes relying on non-formal ways of 'getting by' do indeed have a constraining impact on social mobility. In Barking and Dagenham this is because intergenerational survival strategies have not been dependant upon formal qualifications and academic achievement, hence reducing the likelihood of social mobility. Although the majority of our sample had relatively high career aspirations two years ago, (67 per cent of the sample had ambitions towards a professional/managerial job) subsequent examination results for this the majority of this cohort are disappointing, suggesting that opportunities for the majority to achieve their aspirations are in fact limited. In addition, structural buffers such as a relatively low level of unemployment compared with East London as a whole and a good quality housing stock are supporting the inter-generational survival strategies outlined in this paper. The census and our study data reveal that the locality is not immune to international change. The types of families and households created by Barking and Dagenham residents are becoming more diverse, for example there are now more dual earner households and one-parent households than in the 1950s. However the 'specific circumstances' of Barking and Dagenham's social culture, the continuing strength of kinship structures and cultural support for family life may explain why some of Barking and Dagenham's young people end up being 'conservative' in regard to education and mobility. For the time being at least, cultural and social renewal by other ethnic groups has been minimal and Barking and Dagenham remains a stable enclave of white working class life.

With grateful thanks to pupils, parents and teachers who gave up their time to be involved in the research.

NOTES

1. The proportion of economically inactive men aged sixteen and over for UK is 27 per cent, slightly less than the borough average. The proportion of men in full-time employment in Barking and Dagenham compares favourably with the Greater London average, 49.7 per cent. Economically inactive men (aged sixteen and over) as a percentage of total males: Barking and Dagenham 27.3 per cent, Greater London 24.5 per cent, UK 27 per cent. 1991 Census Report for Inner and Outer London, Parts 1 and 2, 1991 Census General Report for Great Britain, OPCS, Crown Copyright. Economically active men in full-time employment (aged sixteen and over): Barking and Dagenham 50.4 per cent, Greater London 49.7 per cent.

2. GCSE and 'A' Level Examination Results circular - Summer 1994.

3. *Sap* = a foolish person (Concise Oxford Dictionary).

REFERENCES

Annual Abstracts of Statistics, No. 130, G. Dennis (ed), HMSO, London 1994.

Beck, U., *Risk Society*, Sage Publications, London 1992.

Census, 1991 London: Crown Copyright, HMSO.

Hobbs, D., *Doing The Business: Entrepreneurship, the Working Class and Detectives in the East End of London*. Oxford University Press, Oxford 1989.

Hobbs, D., *Bad Business: professional crime in modern Britain*. Oxford University Press, Oxford 1995.

Key Local Authority Statistics, HMSO, London 1993.

London Borough of Barking and Dagenham, *Barking and Dagenham Borough Profile*. London Borough of Barking and Dagenham: Crown Copyright, 1993.

London School Leavers Destinations Survey, The Careers Service, London 1994.

Massey, D. and Allen, J. (eds), *Geography Matters: a reader*, Cambridge University Press, Cambridge 1984.

Mayhew, H., *London Labour and the London Poor*, Volumes 1- 4, Griffin, Bohn and Company, London 1812-1887.

McCarthy, T., *The Great Dock Strike 1889*, Weidenfeld and Nicolson, London 1988.

O'Brien, M and Jones, D., Family Life in Barking and Dagenham. In T. Butler and M. Rustin (eds), *Rising in the East: The Regeneration of East London?*, Lawrence and Wishart, London 1996.

Rix, V., 'Social Change in East London'. In T. Butler and M. Rustin (eds), *Rising in the East: The Regeneration of East London?*, Lawrence and Wishart, London 1996.

Rubinstein, A Andrews, A and Schweitzer, P (eds) (1991) *Just Like The County: Memories of London families who settled the new cottage estates 1919-1939*, Age Exchange, London 1991.

Simmons, M., 'Fresh Script for East Enders', in *The Guardian*, August 14, 1996, pp6-7.

Social Trends, No 24, HMSO, London 1996.

Taylor, I. Evans, K. and Fraser, P., *A Tale of Two Cities: A Study of Manchester and Sheffield*, Routledge, London and New York 1996.

Thompson, P., 'Family Myth, Models and Denials in the Shaping of Individual Life Paths' in D. Bertaux and P. Thompson, *Between Generations: Family Models, Myths and Memories*, Oxford University Press, Oxford 1993, pp13-38.

Tizard, B., Blatchford, P., Burke, J., Farquahar, C. and Plevis, I., *Young Children at School in the Inner City*, Lawrence Erbaum Associates, London 1988.

Willmott, P., *The Evolution of A Community: A Study of Dagenham after Forty Years*, Routledge and Kegan Paul, London 1963.

Young, M. and Willmott, P., *Family and Kinship in East London*, Routledge and Kegan Paul, London 1957.

TRENDS EAST

Industrial decline, economic restructuring and social exclusion in London East, 1980s and 1990s

Vikki Rix

The following trend report outlines and analyses the main effects of economic restructuring and continuing de-industrialisation within the London East sub-region throughout the 1980s and 1990s. This report shows that recent labour market trends and changes within the industrial and occupational structure have impacted on all London East boroughs, particularly pronounced in its effect on Hackney, Tower Hamlets, Newham and Southwark. An inner and outer London East divergence emerges, whereby social and economic exclusion is much more widespread in those districts when compared to the more suburban localities of Dartford, Bexley, Redbridge, Thurrock, Barking and Dagenham and Havering. The prevalence of unemployment, especially amongst young people and ethnic minority groups is discussed as critical social outcomes of our new modern economy.

Since 1979, the neo-liberal ideology of the Conservative government has been implemented in many spheres of social and economic life. The concepts of individualism, indepen-dence and the promotion of the enterprise culture have been strongly advocated as solutions to social and urban regeneration, particularly relevant in London, a major city with multifaceted problems. This philosophy has coincided with deregulation, widespread cuts in public expenditure and the rolling back of the 'Nanny State', as well as continuing de-industrialisation and national economic restructuring. Over the past seventeen years therefore, government policies and the failure of 'trickle-down' economics have contributed to social and economic inequalities, both nationally and in London, particularly eastern areas of London. In charting recent labour market trends, this report

will assess the impact of economic restructuring on the complex and diverse locality of London East, and will also address the growing phenomena of social and economic exclusion within London East communities.[1]

Geographically London East consists of thirteen local authority districts which span both north and south of the River Thames, a region largely corresponding with the eastern Thames corridor. The boroughs representing London East include Hackney, Tower Hamlets and Newham, three racially diverse, deprived Inner London boroughs, Waltham Forest, Redbridge, Barking and Dagenham, Havering and Thurrock. South of the River, London East includes Lewisham, Southwark, Greenwich, Bexley and Dartford.

London and Polarisation

The polarisation of London is not a new issue. On discussing this phenomena, Hall quite aptly described the London East region as

> one of the most remarkably underdeveloped and deprived zones in the affluent South East..........It has a very complex spatial and economic structure, dominated by older extractive and manufacturing and port related industries, housed in settlements that range from small waterside towns...to vast amorphous interwar public housing estates. Its problems are multifold: de-industrialisation, lack of skills for the informational economy, environmental degradation, but above all lack of access (Hall, 1992 p2).

Since the 1970s, largely as a result of economic restructuring and de-industrialisation, the gap between the rich and the poor, the professional and the unskilled, the employed and the unemployed, the housed and the homeless has increased in many major industrialised cities. This concern has been at the forefront of urban social theory and research since the early 1980s, whereby the concept of polarisation has received much attention. Key writers within this field, for example Fainstein *et al* (1992) on London and New York, Sassen (1991) on London, New York and Tokyo, Castells (1989) on US cities and lastly Soja (1988) on Los Angeles, have all similarly investigated both the globalisation of capital and the global restructuring of production, and its associated consequences for individual westernised cities. Global changes in industry and the economy, the increase in service sector occupations, and the introduction of new technology, often referred to as a 'microchip' revolution, have resulted in rising long term unemployment, high rates of youth unemployment, growing economic inactivity and widespread skills mismatch and skills shortages.

This research however, has concentrated on 'major' cities. 'Back Regions' of cities, such as London East, have been neglected (Rustin, 1996) both at a conceptual and analytical level. This report will address this neglect by investigating how major changes within industry and the economy have been constituted in the London East region since the early 1980s. The first section focuses on the main features of industrial decline and economic restructuring within London East, drawing out borough diversity and continuity; the second charts the subsequent changing employment patterns for men and women living in London East. The final section reviews the main social outcomes of economic and industrial change, highlighting the spatial patterns of social and economic exclusion in London East.

The nature of economic restructuring

Following the collapse of post-war Fordism, economies have experienced long term shifts in both modes of production and employment patterns. Throughout the 1970s, mass production and mass consumption declined in many industrialised nations, a decline largely attributed to rising high inflation, the oil shocks of 1974 and 1979 and demands for wage increases in a time of profit reduction. The growing Japanese and American competition, as well as the rise in information technology and new forces of organisation also contributed to high unemployment levels in Britain and most European nations (Kennett, 1994). This coincided with the absolute rise in service sector occupations, especially producer and financial services. Economic transformation was beginning to take place, comprising of three distinct characteristics which have clearly contributed to social and economic polarisation (Penna and O'Brien, 1996). These are: an increase in service sector jobs and a relative or absolute decline in manufacturing industries; the development of core and peripheral work forces; and the transformation in the production and organisation of work and occupations. This next section will assess the impact of these national and international trends on the London East region.

Manufacturing and industrial decline

London East has been an area dominated by heavy industrial and manufacturing employment for many years. This was largely due to the existence of London's docks, which reached the height of success in the immediate post-war period. However, as a result of changing world trade patterns and the collapse of British imperialism, London's docks began to decline and were closed down between 1967 and 1981, beginning with East India Docks and ending with the Royals (Porter, 1994). Between 1971 and 1982 therefore, the proportion of manufacturing jobs fell by 42 per cent, whilst many of the port-related industries such as refineries and dockside handling and processing plants were also closed down in London. The effect on Dockside employment was severe, falling from around 30,000 in the 1950s to a mere 2,000 in 1981 (Porter, 1994). It is true that most major cities have experienced similar trends, but the consequences of economic restructuring have been more pronounced in London, as well as New York. Throughout the 1980s, industrial and manufacturing employment continued to decline across London. Although the free market ideology of Thatcherism and the promotion of business and financial sectors contributed to this decline, other factors such as high costs and congestion, a lack of greenfield sites, and a diminishing input from EU funds also played a part (London; Facts and Figures, 1995). Between 1980 and 1993, manufacturing production dropped from 17 per cent to 12 per cent in London, whilst the proportion of London residents employed in manufacturing industries fell from around a fifth in 1981 to only 11 per cent ten years later.

Since manufacturing and heavy port related industries were the major employers of working class people, it is not surprising that London East boroughs have particularly felt the cost of this decline. It is clear that the shift away from manufacturing industrial employment continued throughout the 1980s. Borough variations however have remained in the 1990s.

Primarily as a result of rises in productivity and falling demand, those boroughs with the highest proportion of employees working in manufacturing generally experienced the largest falls. For example, in Barking and Dagenham manufacturing employment dropped from around 30

Graph 1. Manufacturing decline in London East, 1981-1991

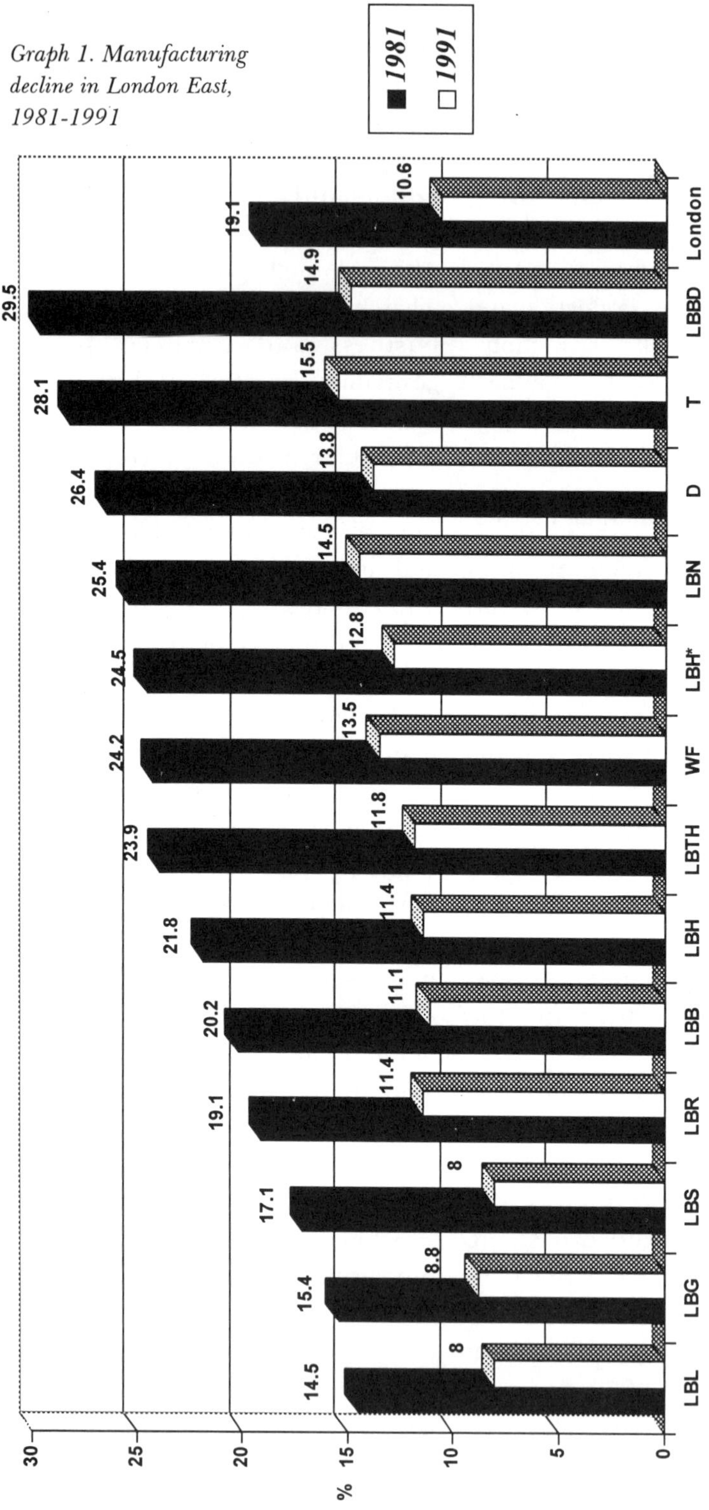

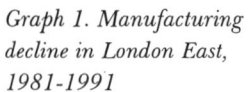

LBL=Lewisham, LBG=Greenwich, LBS=Southwark, LBR=Redbridge, LBB=Bexley, LBH=Hackney, LBTH=Tower Hamlets, WF=Waltham Forest, LBH*=Havering, LBN=Newham, D=Dartford, T=Thurrock, LBBD=Barking&Dagenham

Trends East

per cent in 1981 to 15 per cent in 1991. Similarly, the loss of manufacturing jobs was also high in Thurrock, Dartford, Havering and Tower Hamlets, whose rate of decline ranged from around 12 and 13 per cent - well above the London and national average of 8.5 and 9.2 per cent respectively. In fact only Lewisham, Greenwich and Redbridge had a below London average loss of manufacturing work between 1981 and 1991. Despite the general trend of decline however, London East boroughs, excluding Lewisham, Southwark and Greenwich, still had a higher proportion of residents employed in manufacturing industries compared with London as whole. Again, this was particularly the case in Thurrock, Barking and Dagenham and Newham which had over 14 per cent of residents working in manufacturing, compared to half that in the southern boroughs of Lewisham, Southwark and Greenwich (boroughs which are predominately service sector based).

Summing up, London East boroughs have experienced a continuing decline in manufacturing employment. It has however remained a more significant industrial sector in outer London East, where issues of congestion and greenfield sites are less problematic. Generally London East, especially outer areas, has remained a centre for textiles and printing and still has London's one major car manufacturer operating within its locality, that of Fords in Dagenham (London; Facts and Figures, 1995). Strategically, these may well be valuable assets in preventing further decline in manufacturing and industrial employment in the future.

The rise in service sector employment

Since the late 1970s, the major area of job growth in many western industrialised nations has occurred within services. With regards to London, the increases have been particularly pronounced within the business and financial sector, as well as within the producer and communication services. Despite the damaging economic recession of the early 1990s, London has remained one of the three most important financial centres in the world, along with New York and Tokyo. For example, London's foreign exchange turnover reached $300 billion in 1992 compared to $190 billion in New York and $130 billion in Tokyo (London: Facts and Figures, 1995). Although approximately 100,000 jobs were lost within the service sector between 1989 and 1992, international banking, as well as domestic business and financial services have remained the largest sectors of employment in London. By 1991, 20 per cent of London's resident working population were employed in financial and business services, an increase of 6.7 per cent since 1981. With regards to government and service related industries, nearly a third of London residents were employed in such sectors compared to around 28 per cent in the UK. Throughout the 1980s and early 1990s, the shift from a predominantly industrial to a post-industrial economy continued within the London metropolis. By 1994, 45 per cent of London residents were employed in 'post-industrial' occupations such as social workers, teachers, lawyers, scientists, computer analysts and technicians, compared to the national figure of 35 per cent (London: Facts and Figures, 1995). The inner and outer London divergence has remained because of the bias towards professional and managerial occupations of residents living in areas like Camden, Islington, Hackney, Lambeth, Southwark, Lewisham and more recently Tower Hamlets. In 1994 for example, more than half of inner London's resident population were employed in professional, managerial and technical occupations. By contrast, Outer London is still dominated by clerical and secretarial occupations, where sales and craft related occupations are also more widespread.

Aspects of the new modern economy have also penetrated the London East region. Between 1981 and 1991, all London East boroughs had an increase in the proportion of residents working in banking and finance, as well as government and service related industries (apart from Dartford). However, the shift to a service sector economy has not been a uniform trend across London East; borough diversity has remained and the inner/outer London polarisation is evident. The rise in service sector employment been much more pronounced for local residents living in Tower Hamlets, Hackney, Waltham Forest and Southwark, four localities in close proximity to central London. Throughout the 1980s, Southwark and Tower Hamlets had the highest increases in banking and financial industrial employment, the only two boroughs above the London average rise of 6.7 per cent. By 1991, nearly a fifth of local residents worked in banking and financial industries in Tower Hamlets, Southwark and Lewisham. Bexley, Havering and Redbridge, however, still had the highest proportion of residents working within this sector, the only London East boroughs above the London average of 20.4 per cent.

The distribution of government and service sector employment, however, portrays a rather different London East picture. Throughout the 1980s, the rise in these particular industries far exceeded the London average of 1.8 per cent in Hackney, Tower Hamlets, Waltham Forest and Newham. As a result of high increases, by 1991 over a quarter of Newham residents were employed in government and services, compared to nearly a third in Waltham Forest and Tower Hamlets, and 38.4 per cent in Hackney. Unlike banking and finance employment, the highest proportion of residents working in government and service industries lived in the inner London East boroughs of Hackney, Southwark,

Table 1. Growth in service sector employment, 1981-1991

	% of residents working in		1981 - 1991 increase	
	Banking & Finance	Gov't & Services	Banking & Finance	Gov't & Services
London East Region				
Newham	14.9	27.8	3.4	6.0
Dartford	16.3	26.0	6.3	-2.1
Thurrock	16.3	20.6	5.7	1.7
Barking & Dagenham	16.4	22.8	4.3	3.9
Hackney	16.7	38.4	6.2	7.9
Greenwich	17.5	35.4	5.3	1.5
Waltham Forest	18.1	31.8	6.5	6.3
Tower Hamlets	19.2	32.8	7.0	7.0
Southwark	19.3	37.2	7.1	4.4
Lewisham	19.7	36.1	6.3	2.3
Bexley	20.5	26.8	4.5	0.6
Havering	22.7	23.9	5.9	3.4
Redbridge	23.1	26.7	6.1	1.7
Greater London	20.4	30.7	6.7	1.8
Great Britain	12.0	28.4	4.2	2.2

10% sample.
Source: 1981 and 1991 Census, Crown Copyright.

Lewisham, Greenwich, and Tower Hamlets. By contrast, the lowest proportions were found in Thurrock, Barking and Dagenham and Havering, whilst Dartford actually experienced a decline in service related industrial employment. It is highly probable that the transformation of London's docks into large scale business and financial centres has contributed to the changing industrial and occupational structure of these particular inner London East boroughs. The more recent gentrification of areas like Mile End, Bow, Stepney, Stoke Newington and Upper Leytonstone, where the middle classes are returning and rejuvenating old Victorian and Georgian houses into valuable properties, is also adding to this process of both change and polarisation.

The growth in service sector employment, therefore, has not been uniform across the London East region. Whereas, by 1991, over half of the local residents living in Southwark, Lewisham, Hackney, Greenwich and Tower Hamlets were employed in the service economy,[2] just over a third were working in similar industries in the outer London East areas of Thurrock and Barking and Dagenham. Respective proportions for Newham and Dartford were just over 40 per cent. Within these outer London East boroughs, manual industrial sectors have remained much more significant despite their overall decline. In 1991, over 50 per cent of local residents had remained working in manufacturing, construction, distribution and catering, and transport related industries.

Not surprisingly, continuing de-industrialisation and the new service economy has impacted on the social class composition of London East boroughs. Throughout the 1980s, there has been a general rise in service class occupations, alongside a fairly rapid decline in skilled and unskilled manual occupations, particularly widespread in the inner London East areas. For example, the professionalisation of the work force has been much more pronounced in Tower Hamlets, Southwark, Hackney, Lewisham and Waltham Forest. These boroughs had by far the largest rise in professional and managerial households, which were also above the London average increase of 4.6 per cent. The impact of the financial and property development around the Isle of Dogs was particularly striking, as between 1981 and 1991 the proportion of professional and managerial households nearly doubled in Tower Hamlets, rising from 9 per cent to 17 per cent. By 1991, although most London East boroughs, apart from Barking and Dagenham, Newham, Thurrock, Tower Hamlets and Greenwich, had over a fifth of households consisting of economically active heads working in professional and managerial occupations, they were still below the London average of 27.2 per cent.

Unlike New York, a city experiencing polarisation in terms of occupations,[3] London, especially London East, has seen a fairly dramatic decline in both skilled, partly skilled and unskilled manual occupations. Again, although not surprisingly, the decline in skilled manual, partly skilled and unskilled occupations was exceptionally high in Tower Hamlets, Southwark, Hackney, Lewisham and Newham. It is clearly apparent that, on the one hand, there has been an increase in professional and white collar workers in the inner London East boroughs, but also an increase in those displaced from the labour market due to widespread decline in manual work, contributing to high rates of unemployment and economic inactivity. Earning differentials, and the changing employment patterns for men and women living in London East further supports the polarisation across and within local boroughs.

Earning differentials

Although London East has generally remained a region with low gross weekly earnings for both men and women, wage levels vary considerably across London East. Looking at London as a whole, results from the 1995 New Earnings Survey show that employees in London still earned significantly higher than elsewhere in the UK, with average gross weekly earnings of £498 for full-time males and £349 for full-time females. Despite high unemployment and low economic

Table 2 Average weekly gross earnings for full-time males, London East (rounded to nearest pound)

F-T Males	1990	1991	1992	1993	1994	1995	%change 1991-1995
London East							
Waltham Forest	296	309	338	336	360	-	21.6
Havering	292	328	349	357	378	-	29.4
Lewisham	300	321	337	347	-	376	25.3
Newham	306	343	366	383	374	-	22.2
Greenwich	309	331	351	370	365	381	23.3
Redbridge	319	322	353	381	385	-	20.7
Barking & Dagenham	322	350	365	386	401	418	29.8
Tower Hamlets	388	422	478	535	556	534	37.6
Southwark	391	417	449	460	463	487	24.5
Greater London	383	409	434	461	467	498	30.0
Great Britain	296	319	340	353	362	375	26.7

Table 3 Average weekly gross earnings for full-time females, London East (rounded to nearest pound).

F-T Females	1990	1991	1992	1993	1994	1995	%change 1991-1995
London East							
Greenwich	200	240	261	281	282	294	47.0
Havering	206	238	261	262	283	291	41.3
Lewisham	207	266	-	321	-	-	-
Waltham Forest	211	241	260	246	267	282	33.6
Bexley	213	241	285	260	-	-	-
Redbridge	227	247	279	286	298	316	39.2
Newham	227	255	286	310	308	281	23.8
Tower Hamlets	248	288	322	363	372	379	52.8
Southwark	264	286	313	329	336	349	32.2
Hackney	-	294	-	341	361	359	22.1
Greater London	259	285	309	326	336	349	34.7
Great Britain	201	222	241	253	261	270	34.3

The New Earnings survey data is based upon people working within the local authority area. Where data is not available, sampling error was above 5% and therefore statistically unreliable.
Source: New Earnings Survey.

activity rates, those men and women working full-time in Tower Hamlets earned above London average wages in the early 1990s. The gap has widened since 1991, as the growth in wages has been much higher in Tower Hamlets compared to London and Britain as a whole largely as a result of the increase in professional and other service sector related occupations.

Between 1991 and 1995 male full-time weekly gross earnings rose by 37.6 per cent, compared to 52.8 per cent for women. Female wages also increased at a faster rate than London as a whole in the boroughs of Greenwich and Havering. It is quite clear that economic change has benefited certain sections of both the working and resident communities in Tower Hamlets. The professionalisation of the work force is contributing to rising wages, but at the same time the less skilled, uneducated residents are subject to widespread labour displacement.

In 1994/1995, Waltham Forest, Newham, Havering and Greenwich had the lowest weekly gross earnings for men and women working full time within the London East region. Earning differentials illustrate the diversity of local areas. For example, Barking and Dagenham has remained largely working-class in its industrial and occupational structure and has a poor educational profile. However, it has generally low unemployment levels and high earnings compared to other London East boroughs. In the early 1990s, male full-time earnings were the third highest in London East, and although still below the London average in 1995 surpassed the national average in that year. Skilled manual work has dominated Barking and Dagenham since the 1930s, and the culture of long working hours is still prevalent for many men working in this area in the 1990s. In both 1994 and 1995, men employed full-time in Barking and Dagenham worked the highest number of hours per week (44 hours) and had the highest recorded rate of overtime hours (5.4 and 5.1 overtime hours respectively), both well above the London and national average.

Changing employment patterns and economic risk, London East

So far it is clear that throughout the 1980s, there has been a simultaneous upward and downward drift in opportunities and life chances for London East residents. This pattern of inequality is similarly reflected in the changing employment patterns for men and women living in this region. Throughout the 1980s, the proportion of men participating in the labour market declined in all London East boroughs, a London and nation wide trend. This decline was especially high in Tower Hamlets, Newham, Southwark and Hackney which had the lowest economic activity rates[1] for men in London East, and by 1991 were below the London average of 86.3 per cent. Although the participation of men in the labour force similarly declined in all other London East boroughs, by 1991 they still had higher proportions of economically active men than London as a whole; ranging from 86.9 per cent in Lewisham to the higher proportions of 88 and 90 per cent out in Barking and Dagenham, Havering, Thurrock, Dartford and Bexley.

Table 4. *Proportion of economically active men and women, London East*

	Total Males	1991 % EA	81-91 % change	Total Females	1991 % EA	81-91 Change
London East						
Hackney	56,525	82.5	-5.5	57,068	63.7	-0.1
Tower Hamlets	49,315	82.8	-7.9	46,088	57.0	-5.7
Newham	66,714	83.6	-7.1	63,532	58.9	-1.9
Southwark	68,727	84.6	-5.7	69,247	67.1	-0.01
Lewisham	72,790	86.9	-3.7	73,350	69.6	+2.2
Greenwich	63,103	87.2	-4.4	62,059	66.1	+1.9
Redbridge	71,884	87.4	-3.3	67,947	67.1	+4.0
Waltham Forest	67,679	87.9	-3.8	65,596	68.2	+3.8
Barking&Dagenham	43,236	88.3	-4.7	40,713	64.4	+4.4
Havering	73,344	89.2	-3.6	68,457	67.7	+7.1
Thurrock	41,564	89.4	-3.2	38,866	66.7	+10.4
Dartford	26,378	89.8	-1.6	24,146	70.3	+8.1
Bexley	69,456	90.0	-2.6	65,200	69.7	+6.9
Kent	475,876	88.9	-2.2	439,391	67.0	+9.4
Essex	487,498	89.5	-2.4	450,221	67.4	+9.3
Greater London	2,157,837	86.3	-3.5	2,096,257	67.7	+2.9

EA=Economically Active. Difference in percentage points will have been affected by change in definitions. 1991 Census included students who were also in employment or seeking work in the week before the Census as economically active. 1981 base counts, however, categorised all students as economically inactive.
Source: 1981 and 1991 Census, Crown Copyright.

Perhaps one of the most critical outcomes of economic restructuring has been the dramatic decline in full-time employment for men living in London East boroughs. This decline has coincided with a subsequent increase in men working part-time. The proportion of men working in full-time jobs dropped by over a fifth in all London East districts throughout the 1980s, apart from Thurrock, Dartford, and Barking and Dagenham. The loss of full time jobs was particularly high for men living in Hackney, Newham, Tower Hamlets and Redbridge, which experienced a decline of 25 per cent. As a result, both Hackney and Tower Hamlets had less than half of men aged 16-64 working in full-time jobs by 1991, compared to around 52 per cent in Southwark and Newham. By contrast, the outer London East boroughs still had the highest proportion of men working full-time, ranging from 62 per cent in Barking and Dagenham to 67 per cent in Dartford, compared to the London average of 58 per cent. Although the proportion of men working part-time is still minimal, there has been an overall rise throughout the 1980s. The decline of manufacturing and industrial work, as well as the limited availability of full-time employment, along with the increasing specialisation and flexibility of many professional jobs has contributed to

Table 5. Changing economic characteristics of men living in London East, 1981 - 1991

	1991 percentage of men aged 16-64 employed			1981 - 1991 % Change in		
	F-T	P-T	E.Inactive	F-T	P-T	E.Inactive
London East						
Hackney	45.4	3.7	17.5	-24.8	2.0	5.5
Tower Hamlets	48.5	2.0	17.2	-23.4	0.6	7.9
Southwark	52.1	2.7	15.4	-22.5	1.3	5.8
Newham	52.3	2.1	16.4	-24.3	1.3	7.1
Lewisham	56.6	2.4	13.1	-21.4	1.2	3.7
Redbridge	57.9	2.0	12.6	-24.9	1.0	3.4
Greenwich	58.2	2.0	12.8	-21.6	1.1	4.4
Waltham Forest	59.1	2.1	12.1	-22.0	1.0	3.9
Barking & Dagenham	61.7	1.5	11.7	-19.7	0.9	4.7
Havering	62.8	1.8	10.8	-22.8	1.0	3.6
Thurrock	64.4	1.7	10.6	-16.6	1.1	3.2
Bexley	65.1	1.8	10.0	-20.4	1.0	2.5
Dartford	66.7	1.6	10.2	-17.0	0.9	1.5
Essex	62.6	2.0	10.5	-20.9	1.1	2.4
Kent	62.2	2.1	11.1	-19.9	1.0	2.2
Greater London	57.8	1.9	13.7	-21.9	0.3	4.1

F-T=Full Time, P-T=Part Time, E.Inactive=Economically Inactive. Source: 1981 and 1991 Census, Crown Copyright.

men having to accept part-time employment. It is not surprising that Hackney, Southwark, Lewisham and Newham had the highest proportion of men working in part-time jobs by 1991.

The London-wide trend of growing economic inactivity[5] amongst men also penetrated London East, although to varying degrees. By 1991, Hackney, Tower Hamlets and Newham had nearly a fifth of men aged 16-64 economically inactive, compared with between 10 per cent and 12 per cent ten years earlier. The increase in male economic inactivity was also high in Southwark, rising from 9.6 per cent in 1981 to 15.4 per cent in 1991. By contrast the outer London East boroughs had much lower proportions of economically inactive men ranging between 10 and 12 per cent. It is strikingly clear that men living in Barking and Dagenham, Havering, Thurrock, Bexley and Dartford have been more successful in coping with economic restructuring and the continuing de-industrialisation of local economies. For example, in 1991 those boroughs had the highest economic activity rates for men, the highest proportion of men working full-time, the lowest proportion of economically inactive men and the lowest unemployment levels in both 1991 and more recently in September 1996. Economic and industrial change however, have had a more widespread, damaging effect on men living in inner London East boroughs, men who are more vulnerable to marginalisation and social exclusion.

Changing economic characteristics for women[6]

The inner and outer London East polarisation is similarly apparent with regards to changing employment patterns for women. Between 1981 and 1991, only Tower Hamlets, Newham, Hackney (and Southwark) had a decline in the proportion of women participating in the labour market, compared to the general increase across London and Britain as a whole. Female economic activity rates were again the lowest in those three socially and economically deprived areas[7] and were below the London average of 68 per cent (see Table 4). By contrast, the increase in economically active women was more pronounced in Thurrock, Dartford, Bexley and Havering. This was particularly the case in Thurrock, where in 1981 56.3 per cent of women were economically active; by 1991 this had risen to 66.7 per cent. The proportion of economically inactive women similarly declined by 10.4 per cent. Despite the Docklands redevelopment and the creation of many new non-manual jobs, Tower Hamlets had the lowest proportion of women in the labour force of all

Table 6. Changing economic characteristics of women living in London East, 1981 - 1991.

	1991 percentage of women aged 16-59 employed			1981 - 1991 % Change in		
	F-T	P-T	E.Inactive	F-T	P-T	E.Inactive
London East						
Tower Hamlets	34.2	10.3	43.0	-5.8	-5.5	5.7
Hackney	36.1	10.9	36.3	-5.9	-3.0	0.1
Newham	36.2	10.6	41.1	-3.4	-4.4	1.9
Barking & Dagenham	37.6	19.5	35.6	2.1	-0.8	-4.4
Havering	38.1	22.7	32.3	1.6	1.4	-7.1
Thurrock	38.2	21.4	33.3	5.9	1.7	-10.4
Greenwich	38.9	17.1	33.9	-1.3	-2.5	-1.9
Southwark	40.6	12.2	32.9	-2.8	-5.5	0.0
Redbridge	41.0	16.8	32.9	0.3	-2.1	-4.0
Dartford	41.1	22.3	29.7	4.8	-0.7	-8.1
Bexley	41.2	21.3	30.3	2.1	0.2	-6.9
Waltham Forest	43.3	15.0	31.8	3.0	-4.5	-3.8
Lewisham	44.2	13.7	30.4	0.4	-4.7	-2.2
Essex	36.4	22.8	32.6	3.2	1.2	-9.3
Kent	35.6	22.4	33.0	2.8	1.2	-9.4
Greater London	42.4	14.2	32.3	-0.9	-3.3	-2.3

F-T=Full Time, P-T=Part Time, E.Inactive=Economically Inactive.
Source: *1981 and 1991 Census*, Crown Copyright.

London boroughs (57 per cent), the highest economic inactivity rates for women in London East, 43 per cent compared to 32 per cent in London as a whole, and following the loss of full-time work the lowest proportion of women working in full time employment in 1991. The suggestion that market led regeneration policies have failed to preserve jobs and the existing social structure (Kleinman, 1991) appears justified in Tower Hamlets. This is in contrast with Lakeside in Thurrock where jobs were not only provided but more importantly local people had the appropriate skills for the jobs available. Clerical and secretarial, as well as sales occupations are much more widespread in outer London East. It is not surprising therefore that the highest economic activity rates for women were found in those boroughs.

Changing employment patterns for women living in London East are much more complex. Looking at London as a whole, throughout the 1980s there was a general decline in both female full-time and part-time work, as well as a decline in economic inactivity. However, these trends have not been homogeneous. The loss of full-time employment for women was nearly six times greater than that of London in Hackney and Tower Hamlets, which along with Newham were the only London East boroughs which experienced a rise in economic inactivity amongst women. By contrast, the outer London East boroughs (and Lewisham), had an increase in full-time work, whilst the proportion of women working part-time also increased in Havering, Thurrock, and Bexley. By 1991, the proportion of women working full-time was above the London average of 42.4 per cent in only Lewisham and Waltham Forest. Thurrock and Dartford, which had 38 per cent and 41 per cent of women working in full-time jobs were similarly above the Essex and Kent average in 1991. Part-time employment remained particularly high in the more traditional, predominantly white communities of Havering, Dartford, Bexley and Thurrock, which had over a fifth of women working part-time in 1991 (Barking and Dagenham's figure was also high, 19.5 per cent). However, part-time employment for women was exceptionally low in Tower Hamlets, Newham and Hackney. Interestingly, part-time work for men was geographically the reverse, as the inner London East boroughs had the highest proportion of men working part-time. Growing economic inactivity amongst women only occurred within Tower Hamlets and Newham,[8] where, by 1991, over 40 per cent of women of working age were economically inactive in Tower Hamlets and Newham, 10 per cent above the London average. In summary, economic restructuring and the shift towards to a service sector economy has also had more pronounced effects for women living in inner London East. This was particularly the case in Tower Hamlets,

Hackney and Newham, three inner city areas with a multitude of social and economic problems.

Hard Times; social and economic exclusion in London East

Throughout the 1980s and 1990s, intermittent economic booms and economic recessions have impacted on London East residents in multi-dimensional ways. Alongside an increasing proportion of people becoming owner occupiers, better educated and white collar professional workers, the flip side of the coin has been the increasing marginalisation and exclusion of young school leavers, the uneducated, ex-industrial workers, and ethnic minority groups. Changes within the industrial and occupational structure, whether an incidental or fundamental aspect of modern capitalism (Penna and O'Brien, 1996), have clearly contributed to the dramatic loss of full-time jobs for men, and for women in inner London East boroughs, growing economic inactivity and rising unemployment levels. The free market interventionist policies and changes in social security legislation have also perpetuated levels of social and labour market exclusion amongst local people. The new Job Seekers Allowance for example, which came into operation in October 1996, limits the claiming of unemployment benefit to six months. It also requires a contract to be signed guaranteeing the claimant re-seeking work. This allowance therefore clearly does not take into account the existence of labour market barriers. Despite an overall rise in educational performance throughout the London East region, the problems of de-skilling, skills mismatch, and the lack of highly specialised educational qualifications are still widespread. In fact unemployment trends illustrate that these specific problems have increased with the rise in the informational, technological and knowledge based economy of the 1990s.

As a result of the early 1990s recession, job losses and unemployment in London overtook the national average for the first time in history (Clark, 1996). By 1991, 13.8 per cent and 9.4 per cent of economically active men and women were unemployed in London, compared to 11.3 per cent and 7 per cent in Britain. The impact this has had on London East has been fairly dramatic, as increasingly Central London and City economies have failed to support the employment of London East's unemployed. This has been particularly the case in the inner London East boroughs. The proportion of economically active men unemployed in Hackney and Tower Hamlets rose to over 25 per cent by 1991, twice the London average and was also the second and third highest unemployment rate for men found in all British districts. In Newham and Southwark male unemployment rose to around 22 per cent. A similar trend occurred for economically active women living in inner London East, as the proportion of women unable to find work well exceeded the London unemployment

Table 7. Unemployment levels of economically active men and women, London East, 1981-1991.

	1991 M	% increase 81-91	1991 F	% increase 81-91
London East				
Dartford	8.6	1.1	5.1	0.5
Havering	9.1	1.8	5.3	0.6
Bexley	9.2	2.4	5.9	1.7
Redbridge	10.4	2.7	7.3	1.8
Thurrock	11.2	-0.6	6.4	-1.2
Barking & Dagenham	14.4	2.6	8.4	1.4
Waltham Forest	15.2	4.7	9.6	2.6
Greenwich	16.2	4.3	10.2	3.2
Lewisham	17.6	5.0	11.1	3.5
Southwark	21.6	5.7	14.9	5.9
Newham	22.3	7.6	15.5	5.2
Tower Hamlets	26.3	7.1	15.8	4.8
Hackney	26.4	8.1	18.5	6.1
Greater London	13.8	3.4	9.4	2.4
Great Britain	11.3	-0.2	7.0	-0.7

Source: 1981 and 1991 Census, Crown Copyright.

rate of 9.4 per cent in Southwark, Newham, Tower Hamlets and Hackney. In fact, Hackney's female unemployment rate of 18.5 per cent was the highest of all British districts in 1991. However, unemployment figures in the outer London East boroughs distinctly show that the severity of job losses and diminished job opportunities has been far less severe throughout the 1980s. This was particularly the case in the more affluent suburban areas of Dartford, Havering, Bexley, Redbridge and Thurrock, which had unemployment levels for men and women below the national average in 1991. In fact, Thurrock, like Britain as a whole, actually experienced a decline in the proportion of men and women out of work between 1981 and 1991.

The large scale shopping and retail development at Lakeside has clearly provided jobs for local people living in Thurrock.

More recently, as a result of improvements in the economy, unemployment levels have been decreasing both nationally and within London as a whole. The September 1996 unemployment data for London boroughs however, shows that spatial polarisation of unemployment has remained. Geographically, all outer London boroughs have lower levels of men and women out of work, whilst those boroughs closest to the financial and business centre of London have higher and in some cases exceptionally high unemployment levels. For example, the proportion of men and

Graph 2. Unemployment levels in London East, September 1996.

Source: London Research Centre

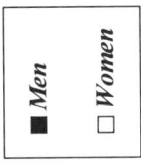

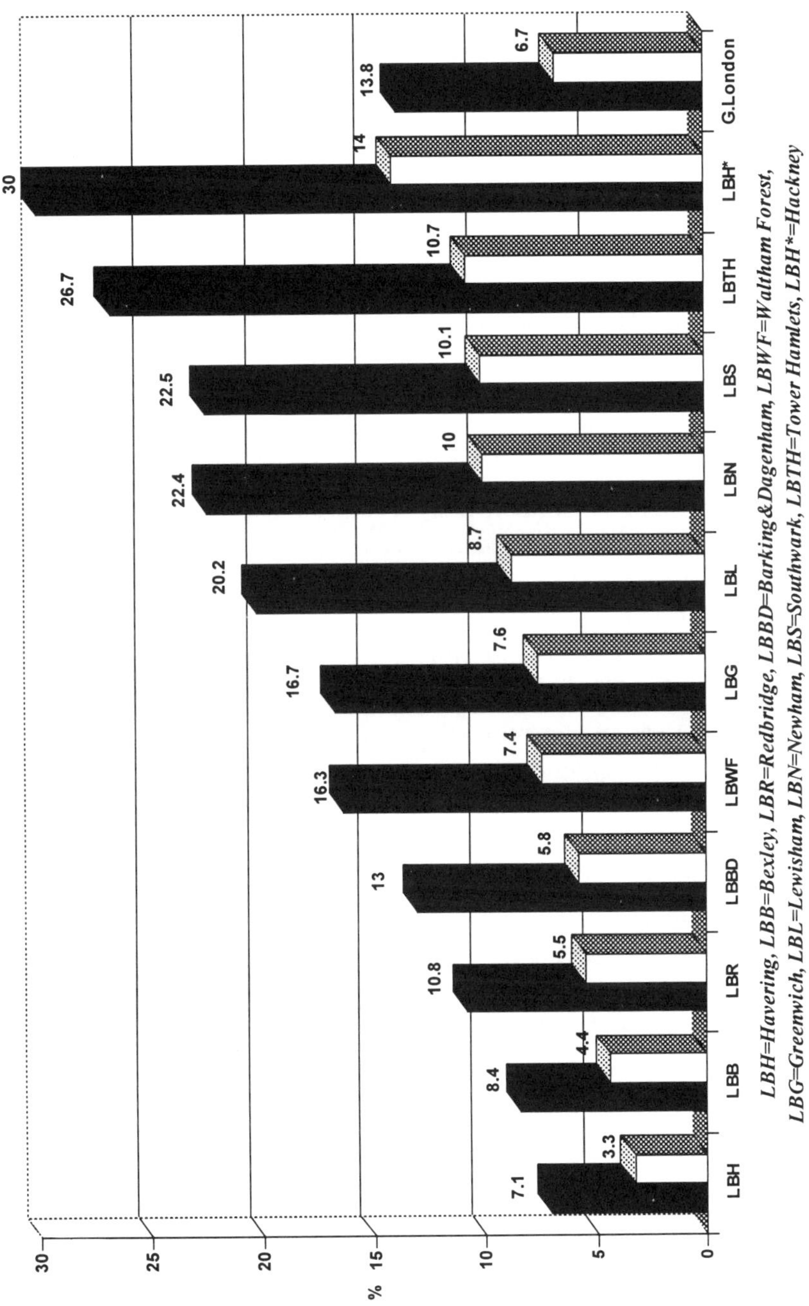

Men
Women
%
0
5
10
15
20
25
30
LBH
LBB
LBR
LBBD
LBWF
LBG
LBL
LBN
LBS
LBTH
LBH*
G.London
7.1
3.3
8.4
4.4
10.8
5.5
13
5.8
16.3
7.4
16.7
7.6
20.2
8.7
22.4
10
22.5
10.1
26.7
10.7
30
14
13.8
6.7
LBH=Havering, LBB=Bexley, LBR=Redbridge, LBBD=Barking&Dagenham, LBWF=Waltham Forest,
LBG=Greenwich, LBL=Lewisham, LBN=Newham, LBS=Southwark, LBTH=Tower Hamlets, LBH*=Hackney

women unemployed in September this year had remained very high in the inner London East boroughs of Hackney, Tower Hamlets, Southwark, Newham and Lewisham. These particular local areas have large numbers of young children and young adults, and are also much more racially and culturally diverse when compared to other London boroughs. As was the case back in the early 1980s and 1990s, the outer London East boroughs, especially Bexley and Havering still had much lower levels of both men and women out of work.

Impact of ethnicity and racial diversity

It is clear that the inner London East boroughs have certainly accumulated a disproportionate share of the unemployed and the economically inactive, trends closely associated with ethnic diversity and the more recent arrival of new immigrants and refugees. Ethnic diversity is a significant issue when investigating both polarisation and social exclusion, as immigration and ethnicity have been key features of both London's and particularly London East's history over the past century. This is also because the proportion of non-white residents varies tremendously between the London East districts. For example, in 1991, over a third of residents were in ethnic groups other than white in Newham, Hackney and Tower Hamlets. Respective figures for Southwark, Lewisham, Waltham Forest and Redbridge were between 20 per cent and 26 per cent. By contrast, the southern and northern outer suburban areas of Bexley, Barking and Dagenham, Dartford, Thurrock and Havering are still predominantly white, having between 93 per cent and 98 per cent of white residents back in 1991. The ethnic and cultural diversity of the inner London East boroughs has continued with the arrival of new ethnic communities such as Somalian refugees and Bangladeshis, particularly in Tower Hamlets and Newham. Certain ethnic groups are more at risk of social and economic exclusion, as a result of both cultural barriers and language problems. High ethnic unemployment rates clearly show that black and Asian people, unlike in the 1950s and 1960s, can no longer simply be assimilated into industrial and manufacturing employment. This is also the scenario for many of the young white working-class, who leave school at sixteen with low educational qualifications. As already stated, the new modern economy requires a highly qualified work force. Although ethnic minority groups are increasingly becoming better qualified, racial discrimination in the labour market is well documented, and non-English speaking immigrants are obviously going to be more at risk of exclusion from work.

It is not surprising therefore, correlating with national trends, that within the inner and outer London East boroughs unemployment is exceptionally high for both Bangladeshi and Pakistani, as well as black African residents. In Newham and Tower Hamlets for example, over 40 per cent of economically active Bangladeshis were unemployed in 1991, compared to 39 per cent in Hackney, and a third in Southwark and Waltham Forest. Similarly, over a quarter of economically active Pakistani residents were out of work in Waltham Forest and Barking and Dagenham, figures above the London average of 24 per cent. Black African unemployment was also particularly high in Newham (reaching nearly 40 per cent), Tower Hamlets and Hackney. Not surprisingly, unemploy-ment levels amongst white, black African, black Caribbean, Pakistani and Bangladeshi residents were generally the highest in Newham, Southwark, Tower Hamlets and Hackney, boroughs which have been most affected, as already shown, by economic restructuring.

Young people and unemployment

Perhaps one of the most substantial outcomes of economic and industrial change has been rising youth unemployment, an international, national and local phenomenon. Within the European Union, for example, youth unemployment rose from 15 per cent to 21 per cent between 1990 and 1994, although strong national variations have persisted (Employment in Europe, 1994).[10] As a result of changes in the market, and the greater flexibility and specialisation of service occupations, there has been a real scarcity of appropriate jobs for many young people leaving school throughout the 1980s. In Britain the Social Security Act of 1988, which raised the age of claiming unemployment benefit from sixteen to eighteen, clearly contributed to the difficulties, both financial and emotional, of young people trying to find work. This was certainly the case in London, a city serviced by business and financial, as well as professional occupations. By 1991, a quarter of economically active men aged between sixteen and nineteen were unemployed in London, compared to nearly a fifth of men aged twenty to twenty-four. Respective figures for young women were also high, 20 per cent and 12 per cent respectively.

The situation facing school leavers and young people living in London East was also rather depressing throughout the 1980s. By 1991, the proportion of young people unemployed was exceptionally high and above the London average in many London East boroughs, especially for those aged between sixteen and nineteen. The spatial patterns of young people's exclusion from the labour market also correlates with the overall polarisation between inner and outer London East. Young people living in close proximity to the service and informational economy of Central London were much more at risk of economic exclusion. By 1991 for example, Lewisham, Tower Hamlets, Southwark, Newham and Hackney had

Table 8. Rising unemployment for young men, 1981 - 1991.

% of economically active men aged 16-19 and 20-24 unemployed

	Aged 16-19 %unemployed	% 81-91 change	Aged 20-24 %unemployed	% 81-91 change
London East Region				
Dartford	16.5	1.6	13.6	2.8
Havering	17.1	3.6	14.7	4.7
Bexley	17.9	3.5	14.1	4.1
Thurrock	20.7	0.8	14.3	-0.8
Redbridge	20.1	4.1	15.8	4.3
Barking & Dagenham	25.5	8.0	19.1	3.5
Waltham Forest	28.9	10.6	20.6	6.2
Greenwich	27.9	6.1	23.1	6.6
Lewisham	31.7	7.6	24.2	7.1
Tower Hamlets	34.4	11.3	26.8	7.3
Southwark	35.3	9.1	28.0	7.6
Newham	35.7	11.6	29.1	11.2
Hackney	41.4	12.0	33.8	11.5
Greater London	25.8	6.5	19.3	5.2
Kent	18.5	1.2	14.6	1.1
Essex	17.9	2.6	13.6	1.4

Source: 1981 and 1991 Census, Crown Copyright.

Table 9. Rising unemployment for young women, 1981 - 1991.

% of economically active women aged 16-19 and 20-24 unemployed

	Aged 16-19 %unemployed	% 81-91 change	Aged 20-24 %unemployed	% 81-91 change
London East Region				
Havering	11.7	2.9	7.8	1.5
Dartford	12.8	2.8	6.9	1.0
Bexley	12.8	3.4	8.3	2.6
Thurrock	14.6	-1.7	7.9	-3.2
Redbridge	16.0	4.1	10.7	3.3
Barking & Dagenham	20.1	5.8	10.3	1.0
Waltham Forest	21.5	6.6	13.3	4.0
Greenwich	24.4	10.4	15.2	3.7
Lewisham	24.6	5.1	16.0	6.2
Southwark	27.9	7.1	19.0	6.8
Newham	28.5	7.3	21.1	8.3
Tower Hamlets	31.4	10.0	18.3	4.7
Hackney	32.2	7.7	24.4	8.4
Greater London	19.8	4.6	12.5	6.1
Kent	14.2	-1.1	9.0	-0.4
Essex	13.2	0.8	8.2	0.0

Source: 1981 and 1991 Census, Crown Copyright.

very high rates of youth unemployment, reaching 35 per cent and 41 per cent for men aged between sixteen and nineteen in Southwark, Newham and Hackney. Reversing this tide of extreme exclusion has to become the centre of any economic and urban regeneration strategy. The movement from school to employment represents one of the most significant transitional periods for young people. Not only does it represent a time of financial independence from the family, but is also a period of social and emotional development whereby new networks are established. Being unemployed at such an early age, along with the current lack of sufficient and appropriate local jobs, is disrupting the social and psychological development of young people who are increasingly displaying anomie and disintegrative tendencies. This is particularly within the realm of drugs and other spheres of the informal economy. Widespread poverty and homelessness amongst young people living in inner city areas is also certainly on the rise.

By contrast, unemployment for young men and women was lower than the London average in the majority of the outer London East boroughs. Young people in Bexley, Havering, Redbridge and Dartford have been much more successful in securing employment throughout the 1980s, experiencing very small increases in unemployment during this period. In fact, Thurrock experienced a decline in unemployment for young women of both age groups and for those men aged twenty to twenty-four. It is highly probable that Lakeside has contributed to the inclusion of young people into local labour markets, whilst the failure of Docklands and its neglect of the local skills mismatch has been well documented.

Conclusion

Overall, this report has revealed widespread economic and industrial change penetrating the London East region. This has however been more profound in its effects in the inner city areas of Hackney, Tower Hamlets, Newham and Southwark, than that experienced by Barking and Dagenham, Havering, Thurrock, Dartford and Bexley. An inner and outer London East divergence has clearly emerged when analysing the effects of economic restructuring, a diversity that continues to illustrate the heterogeneity of London East boroughs. It is clear that throughout the 1980s people living and working in London East have been faced with an increasing situation of both opportunity and risk. Looking at the issue of risk, it has been shown that economic transformation has widened the social and economic divisions both within and across London East boroughs. Those people more at risk of marginalisation and exclusion, largely as a result of economic and industrial change, predominantly live in the inner London East boroughs, and consist of the growing number of people out of work (particularly high for young people and ethnic minority groups) the economically inactive and finally those men who experienced a rapid loss of full-time work throughout the 1980s.

As Rustin (1996) states, to conceptualise and promote London East only as a region of social and economic problems, a widely held perception of the area, is not only negative but is also narrow. It would, however, be equally unrealistic to under play some of the immediate problems London East must overcome before it becomes a region of equal opportunities and equal life chances for all those who live and work there. Having examined and highlighted the main outcomes of economic restructuring throughout the London East region, it is clear that new focused strategies need to be developed, strategies that enable the majority of people to compete equally in our new modern economy. This is vital for the reversal and prevention of further social and economic exclusion throughout the London East region in the next millennium.

NOTES

1. The 1981 and 1991 Census returns are the primary source of data for this analysis. The Census is still the major comprehensive source of social and economic material at the local authority level.

2. The Service economy includes banking and finance industries, as well as government and service-related industries.

3. Sassen has shown that in New York there has been both an increase in service class occupations, as well as lower working-class occupations.

4. The economically active population includes employees, self-employed, persons on a government or training scheme and the unemployed (seeking work) for those men aged 16-64 and women aged 16-59. The 1991 Census included students, who were employed or seeking work, as economically active.

5. Economically inactive includes; students without a job in the week prior to the 1991 Census, permanently sick people, retired people, and people looking after the home or family and not in paid employment.

6. A more detailed analysis of women's work and the apparent feminisation of the labour market in London East will be provided in a forthcoming issue.

7. This is due to low economic activity rates amongst different ethnic minority women.

8. Hackney's rise in economically inactive women was marginal.

9. The 1991 Census of Population introduced a question on ethnicity for the first time.

10. Youth unemployment is exceptionally high in Greece, France, Italy and Spain. For example in 1994 respective figures were, 28 per cent, 29.5 per cent, 32.1 per cent and 45% per cent.

REFERENCES

Castles, M., *The Informational City*, Blackwell, Oxford 1989.

1981 Census, HMSO, Crown Copyright, London.

1991 Census, HMSO, Crown Copyright, London.

Clark, C., 'East London and Europe' in *Rising in the East: The Regeneration of East London*, Lawrence and Wishart, London 1996.

Fainstein, S. Gordon, I. and Harloe, M., *Divided cities: New York and London in the contemporary world*, Blackwell, Oxford 1992.

Hall, P., 'A New Strategy for the South East', *The Planner*, 22nd March 1993.

Kennett, P., 'Exclusion, post-Fordism and the "New Europe"' in *A New Europe? Economic Restructuring and Social Exclusion*, UCL Press, London 1994.

Kleinman, M., 'Housing and urban politics in Europe: towards a new consensus?' in *A New Europe? Economic Restructuring and Social Exclusion*, UCL Press, London 1991.

London: Facts and Figures, 1995 Edition, HMSO, London, Crown Copyright.

London Research Centre, *Population Change in London 1981-1991*, HMSO, London 1993.

Penna, S. and O'Brien, M., 'Postmodernism and Social Policy: A Small Step Forwards?', *Journal of Social Policy*, Volume 25, 1, 1996, pp39-61.

New Earnings Survey, HMSO, London.

Porter, R., *A Social History of London*, Hamish Hamilton, London 1994.

Rustin, M., 'Perspectives on East London' in *Rising in the East: The Regeneration of East London*, Lawrence and Wishart, London 1996.

Sassen, S., *The Global City: New York, London, Tokyo*, Princeton University Press, Princeton, NJ 1991.

Soja, E., *Postmodern Geographies*, Verso, London 1988.

ARTY FACTS

The Talking Cure

Harold Pinter and the voices of East End writers

Ken Worpole

Cities are as much imaginary constructions as they are economic entities, and few parts of the world have been as endlessly re-imagined as London's East End. Its symbolic status within the wider English, or British, sense of identity has alternated between representing a degraded 'other', a fearsome, corrupt, brutalised and seditionary quarter of the capital, and the 'lousy but loyal', deeply patriotic bulldog spirit of the blitz, with its spontaneous cockney knees-ups beneath the naphtha flares. Its richness as a source of fictional representation is mostly attributable to two things: a brooding, riparian architecture encroached upon by a maze of ethnic ghettos, markets and tenements, and its demotic, hybridised speech. Get these two things half right: a bit of local geographical detail and a few dropped aspirants, and the work of the jobbing writer is almost done.

The fascination with this part of London seems almost universal. The soap opera, 'EastEnders', has become a nightly surrogate organic community for nearly a quarter of all those living in the United Kingdom, itself a geographical and political settlement that is beginning to look less functional than many of its urban centres, a tribute to the ability of cosmopolitan cities and districts to weather social and cultural change better than nation-states. East London's most flavoursome historian and commentator, Bill Fishman, happily still alive and still perambulating, has noted on more than one occasion the remarkable continuity of the area's cosmopolitan, chaotic and hard-pressed culture, evidence anew of the area's synchronistic circularity - the more things change the more they stay the same. However if you want an antidote to Fishman's enthusiastic and celebratory cadences, then a couple of evenings spent reading the late Dr David Widgery's last, and finest, book, *Some Lives*, will convince you that not only is the East End in a state of enormous social disrepair, but that the worst is yet to come. Neither point of view is necessarily truer than the other.

The literature of the East End (and for the purposes of this essay I have included Hackney in this cultural geography), is a particularly strong and rich body of work, and has powerful topographical elements. Arthur Morrison's *Tales of Mean Streets* (1894) was written after the success of his single story, *The Street*, which appeared in a London magazine in 1891, and is regarded as one of the founding documents of the 'Cockney School'. In this documentary story, the single street is taken to represent a whole life, culture and universe - of poverty, want and brutality, allied to a mordant humour. His most famous novel, *Child of the Jago* (1896), is based on a small area of Bethnal Green, where Arnold Circus now stands, called 'The Jago' in the novel, but known as Old Nichol in real life, a world wholly self-contained and brutal. At this time, two other writers, H.M. Tomlinson and W.W. Jacobs, both enormously popular at the end of the nineteenth century were writing maritime and ghost stories largely based in and around Shadwell and the Isle of Dogs, with much invocation of dripping fogs, the gloom created by the high dock walls, and the story-telling propensities of sailors, lightermen and dockers in various waterfront inns. For a period the ghost story in Britain was very closely associated with London's riverside, particularly in and around the Pool of London.

With the arrival of a distinctive East End Jewish novel-writing culture in the 1930s, the locus of the writing, understandably, moved away from the river and to the tenement blocks, sweat shops, synagogues, public baths, public libraries, and various Jewish cultural institutions and meeting places close to Whitechapel. For writers such as Simon Blumenfield, Willy Goldman, Emmanuel Litvinoff and Ashley Smith, as well as earlier poets and artists such as Isaac Rosenberg, David Bomberg and Mark Gertler, social and cultural life revolved around the Whitechapel Library, the Yiddish Theatre in Commercial Road, and the Workers' Circle Club in Alie Street, as well as a number of cafes and billiard halls.

These places still have something of a contemporary resonance, in quite different circumstances, since there are currently talks about completely revamping the sadly neglected Whitechapel Library, restoring it once again to its earlier cultural pre-eminence in East End life. Although now closed, the Half Moon Theatre, which opened in Alie Street in the 1970s in the synagogue building opposite the Workers' Circle Club, and was for a number of years responsible for a terrific flow of theatre-writing, acting and directing talent, continued that tradition, as does the still thriving Eastside bookshop in Whitechapel Road, publishing the stories and poems of newer generations. The

Freedom Press bookshop still operates from nearby Angel Alley, a redoubt of anarchist politics which has always had a firm footing in the area.

More recent writers exploring this beleaguered terrain, notably Iain Sinclair and, to a lesser extent, Peter Ackroyd, have gone underground, evoking a subterranean world of church crypts, lost cemeteries and plague burial grounds, asylum gardens, marshlands and sewage outfalls, hidden rivers, canals and baroque, murderous cosmologies, in order to underpin the modern East End with what they properly regard as its violent and necro-romantic past. Sinclair's *Downriver* is a wonderful achievement and already a permanent fixture in the literature of the East End, but the more recent *Radon's Daughters* is to my mind virtually unreadable, at least when sober.

Two playwrights, Bernard Kops and Arnold Wesker (especially the latter) have also celebrated this contingent, energetic but only sporadically well-lit world of East End street life and politics, but it is Harold Pinter who has achieved a universal resonance for a language and a sensibility that was almost wholly formed in the streets and austere interiors of post-war Hackney, particularly Clapton and Dalston. Pinter's world has become almost as universal as that of Kafka, or Beckett, in the sense that he has created an aesthetic and a cosmos that is instantly identifiable and seems to transcend cultural and national boundaries. Yet he has done this through the adoption of a minimalist programme, a highly filtered world evoking 'traditional' East End mores and registers, but which like an icy wind, reduces the world to an elemental state of being.

A recent biography of Pinter, by *The Guardian*'s theatre critic, Michael Billington,[1] provides a useful chronology and exposition of the plays, and some useful early biographical detail, but is largely uncritical, and weak on the wider cultural context of the world in which Pinter grew up, and at times misses the main story altogether. Take one example, the apparently arbitrary choice of Pinter's stage name, David Baron, which Pinter in retrospect remembers as being the maiden name of a half-forgotten grandmother. It is almost impossible to believe that Pinter did not know of the work - and therefore the name - of the enormously popular, and very fine, Hackney novelist, Alexander Baron, whose war novel, *From the City, From the Plough* (1948), sold more than a quarter of a million copies, and remains one of the most moving novels about World War Two. As a result of the publication of *From the City, From the Plough*, Baron became a famous Hackney writer, another Jew who, like Pinter, had espoused atheism and bohemian and political dissent, and who carried on writing novels, some of which, such as the marvellous *Lowlife* (1961) were set in Hackney. (The precise location of the main action in *Lowlife* is Foulden Road, the author once told me, which is less than ten minutes' walk from Pinter's parents' home in Thistlethwaite Road). Baron was at the height of his fame when Pinter was still living in Hackney, yet he gets no mention in Billington's book.

The book does provide some biographical information, however, which genuinely illuminates Pinter's strong relationship between topography and *mentalité*, between place-names and their immediate evocation of a distinct sensibility and aura. For example we learn that one of Pinter's fondest - and therefore formative - memories is of regular outings with his then English teacher at Hackney Downs School, Joe Brearley. 'We embarked on a series of long walks, which continued for years, starting from Hackney Downs, up to Springfield Park, along the River Lea, back up Lea Bridge Road, past Clapton Pond, through Mare Street to Bethnal Green.' On their walks they would 'declaim passages from Webster into the wind or at passing trolley buses.'

The perambulatory mode is one of the distinguishing features of a certain kind of male writing about the East End. This is a different kind of walking entirely from that of the strolling *flâneur*. The twentieth century urban fabulist strides the streets, parks, underpasses, towpaths, buffeted on all sides by the wind, indifferent to the sun or rain. Iain Sinclair has on several occasions claimed that most of his fictional divination is done on long night-walks through the gloomier parts of the East End, and in a recent review of Peter Ackroyd's book on William Blake, described how he'd set about testing the veracity of Ackroyd's topographical knowledge by walking the streets late at night for several weeks in the distant hope of bumping into Ackroyd doing the same. 'Bowling along' the streets of Hackney seemed to have been one of Pinter's favourite pastimes, usually accompanied by a small group of close male friends. It was often on such walks that he picked up an early apprehension of that mixture of concern and menace which was latent in the apparently artless exchanges which passed between gangs of men, and even individuals, hanging about in the empty, darkened streets, or at late night coffee stalls. 'All right, then?' 'Yeah, fine, thanks. You all right?' 'Yeah, fine.' 'Well that's all right, then.'

Billington's biography reminds us, though not in sufficient detail or depth in my opinion, of the debt owed by Pinter to some of the traditions of music hall, television comedy and even game shows, with which East End popular culture is now inextricably entwined. For example, there is a long tradition of male double acts, in which one partner plays a scheming spiv or conman, and the other a simple dupe or fall guy. There has often been a conscious degree of cruelty and menace in many of these relationships and exchanges. Billington mentions music hall comedians, Jewel & Warriss, and

TV comedians Tony Hancock and Syd James in this regard. But we should not forget the tense, destructive relationship of Harold Steptoe and his father, or, at its most extreme, the double act of Alfred Marks and Nicholas Parsons, popular on television in the 1960s, in which the former often played a scheming tramp with no redeeming features at all, and in which the comedy was thoroughly bleak and bitter, and heavy with malevolent power and deliberate humiliation. This genre of street-wise black and white comedy sketches, with its junkyard and park bench settings, or gloomy kitchen sink interiors, shared more than just stage sets with the early television plays of Pinter presented by Granada's *Armchair Theatre*, and which galvanised, perplexed and sometimes horrified a nation.

Pinter was also struck by the cynical bullying evident in many of the game shows in which bumptious quiz-masters tried to trick contestants with a rapid-fire set of questions to which they were not allowed to answer a simple yes or no without forfeiting their winnings. A number of the early plays - *The Dumb Waiter, The Birthday Party, The Caretaker* - were essentially interrogation scenes between changing alliances of men with no apparent loyalties, sometimes comic, sometimes bristling with fear and dumb terror.

If Pinter took some of the psycho-dynamics and stage sets of his early plays from music hall, television situation comedy and even second rate theatrical whodunnits (as a young actor he had toured in Agatha Christie plays and matinee melodramas), his use of language was from the first uniquely his own. Pinter's characters often speak at cross purposes, they frequently never finish their sentences, their exchanges are full of *non sequiturs*: in short, linguistically, they never connect. In total contrast to a writer like Steven Berkoff, who has elaborated East End demotic into a baroque, florid phantasmagoria, Pinter has reduced the vernacular to an arbitrary collection of left-overs and throwaways from fully formed communication.

In trying to understand Pinter's achievement, I think we can learn much from the anthropological development of 'rubbish theory', an attempt to explain how cultural value is attributed or denied to artefacts and ideas, sometimes in completely arbitrary ways. Rubbish theory seeks to explain, for example, how objects are divided up into transient, durable and disposable categories, some gaining in value over time, some losing value over time, and some seemingly never having any value at all. These are not hard and fast categories for all time, as last century's ephemera can suddenly become immensely valuable to today's collectors, and objects and ideas which were once thought to have been of timeless value, can to later generations seem ridiculous or worthless. Rubbish theory is also related to anthropological notions of the sacred and the profane, or purity and impurity, in which it is the social and cultural context that ascribes value, rather than inherent worth, famously formulated as the notion that dirt is 'matter in the wrong place'. The speech of Pinter's characters is ostensibly ephemeral - cheap, degraded, inconsequential, poorly constructed - and yet in the right settings takes on all kinds of ambiguous and latent meanings, rendering it at times as precious as jewels. Even silence becomes of enormous significance and worth.

This is Pinter's great achievement, to have decisively moved away from traditional stage speech, particularly from conventional 'Cockney' registers and rhetorics, demonstrating that speech is not 'a thing apart' from the body or the physical presence of the character. His best plays reveal that in these apparently inarticulate, unsuccessful exchanges between people, there are whole worlds of meaning and inference, lifetimes of unhappiness, guilt or yearning. To this extent, Pinter's universalising of a speech world that had previously been regarded as second-order, ephemeral, banal - the small change of an already devalued currency - is a remarkable, and radical, aesthetic achievement.

Since those early Hackney plays, Pinter has moved away, geographically and socially. The theatre curtains now often open on to well-upholstered rooms in country house settings - with the distant roar of the sea in the background, a recurring allusion to Pinter's memories of being evacuated to Cornwall during the war - but the human predicament remains the same: the struggle for power and ascendancy in changing configurations of intimate relationships. Pinter has also written much more directly political plays, or directed the work of other more ostensibly political writers, especially where the dominant issues are of the suppression of language and identity through brute force or psychological forms of torture or abuse, invariably portrayed at the level of direct personal confrontation between accusers and accused, perpetrator and victim, those who control and those who are to be controlled.

Pinter long ago left behind the social realism or moral abstractions of Wesker and Kops, as well as eschewing the new Elizabethan rough music of Berkoff. A Pinter play is now *sui generis*, instantly recognisable, even though there are no longer any detailed indications of place, time or psychological verisimilitude. The recent première of *Moonlight* at the Almeida Theatre, strayed across generations, actual or alleged familial and sexual relationships, even alluding to some kind of communication between the living and the dead, with complete confidence, yet also a heart-breaking sense of loss. Even though its principal characters were an elderly, middle-class couple, still to the end uncertain as to whether they had really ever loved each other, beneath the well polished truisms and highly modulated exchanges, quite violent and crude emotions were only partly successfully kept in check. Time and again Pinter reaches into his memory or unconscious to allay the ghosts of his childhood memories, vague intimations of a bleakness and hard struggle for survival that is still quite evident even today in the 'wastes' of Kingsland Road and Whitechapel, or along the battle-scarred shopfronts and breeze-blocked voids of Mare Street: not so much a place but a combative and yet occasionally, it has to be said, hopeless state of mind.

1. Billington M., *The Life and Work of Harold Pinter*, Faber & Faber, London 1996.

Having a wonderful time

On developing a visitor economy for East London

Bruce Jerram & Richard Wells

Vision or mirage?

Over the past few years in East London, tourism projects and visitor-related ventures galore and on the grandest scale have sprung up to bid for all the new and tantalising pots of investment cash. Funding sources have included the Lottery Fund, the Millennium Fund, City Challenge and Single Regeneration budgets, European Union Structural Funds, Private Finance Initiatives and commercial partners. The bids have met with very considerable success. A momentum is gathering, so that hardly a week now seems to go by without the announcement of substantial funding secured for some tourism-related bid, or without proposals being put forward for yet another major tourist attraction in East London.

The rhetorics, rationales, and assumptions underlying these individual developments have rapidly begun to constitute a new, and totally unexpected prospect for the East London region. Yet this projected future as a whole has so far made no comparable bid for public attention. Its implications for the entire region have hardly been acknowledged, its viability and desirability have not yet been subject to consideration and debate. This article will attempt to open up some of the issues for public discussion.

It may well be that this particular vision of East London has not come into public focus because it is so recent, or is still only implicit: a shifting kaleidoscope of piecemeal, opportunistic and competing initiatives which have yet to coalesce into a recognisable pattern in the visual cortex of the body politic. It may also be that the vision being created overall seems so incongruous that no-one really believes in it, beyond its rhetorical, local usefulness to attract funding to a particular project. Or that once fully imagined, it raises so many daunting, contentious and complex issues that no-one really wants to try and think them through.

For it is a vision of East London receiving tens of millions of freely-spending visitors, who have a wonderful time across a region-wide network of flagship attractions and lively, distinctive and convivial neighbourhoods. As well as people on a day's outing from their homes in the locality and region, there are millions from the rest of the country and from overseas who stay locally in a wide variety of accommodation which meets their needs and expectations. The visitors part with billions of pounds which provide well-paid, full-time and acceptably regular employment for a significant proportion of the region's resident population, who are welcoming, skilled and entrepreneurial.

There is a positively millenarian intensity to this dream which has been engendered through the competitive feeding frenzy at the intoxicating streams of urban regeneration funding. It is a dream of pleasure domes and palaces; leisure-craft plying the sacred Thames; an efflorescence of the arts; theme parks, sporting spectaculars and activity centres; thriving cosmopolitan street markets; festivals and fun among the stadia, shopping emporia and restaurants; blessed peace and tranquillity among the forests, wetlands and nature reserves.

Well, we said it might seem an incongruous vision for East London, which is at present almost as remote from the tourism economies of Florida, or Tuscany or the Paris region as it is from an imaginary realm of Xanadu. It is the nature of these incongruities which we wish to explore: the conflicting perceptions, aspirations and values; the vast economy developing from a minimal base; the confident projections when so much is in flux; the incommensurate time scales; the perplexities of spatial definition and location. For it is a plain fact that this vision will have to come into realistic focus, and its drastic demands grappled with in entirely practical ways, if so many current developments and proposals, and so much public effort and investment, are to make any sustainable sense as a regeneration programme for the region.

It is no easy matter even to gather information on the proliferation and shifting fortunes of all the major projects and schemes, which together imply such a vision. The schemes are promoted in a largely localised context, while the rationales and assumptions behind them are of global dimensions. Firstly, what particular projects are in prospect?

The local projects

Most notably of all, there has been the announcement that the northern tip of the Greenwich peninsula is to be the chosen site for the National Millennium Exhibition. The investment required amounts to around £700 million, with the exhibition to be based around a spectacular Millennium Dome. Current uncertainties about funding arrangements notwithstanding, twelve million visitors to the site are officially anticipated when it opens for the year 2000.

At the Greenwich National Maritime Museum a few miles away, the 'Neptune Court Project' involves a £20 million plan to completely renovate the displays and create in effect an entirely new museum. A number of other initiatives, led principally by the Greenwich Waterfront Partnership, have recently come together to enhance the borough's tourism role, including plans for a whole complex of military museums based within the magnificent architecture of the Woolwich Royal Arsenal. The South-East London Tourism Initiative is designed to consolidate a tourism economy with major development plans right down into the Kent part of the Thames Gateway.

On the other side of the Thames from Greenwich, among the Inner Docks, the Docklands Arena has already been built as a vast entertainment and indoor sports venue. This is adjacent to the stupendous Canary Wharf office development complex, and the Docklands Visitor Centre. A new Museum of Docklands is now proposed for West India Quay. In the so far undeveloped watery wastes of the outer Royal Docks, the massive new International Exhibition Centre is planned for a site beside the Royal Victoria Dock. London Zoo has proposed a £100 million National Aquarium attraction nearby. The Royal Albert Dock is being proposed as a national watersports centre with an Olympic rowing course and, even as we write, we hear that £9 million has just been awarded to the scheme.

London's local authorities have been urged to take tourism needs into account when developing local planning policies and some East London boroughs are displaying a commitment to attracting visitors. The

'Hackney 2000' regeneration programme places a particular emphasis on the visual arts and crafts, and Hackney is attempting to develop a lively 'city fringe' economy in association with Tower Hamlets, including a Developing Cultural Quarters Project. Waltham Forest stands out for having an agreed and published Tourism Strategy. A 26 kilometre corridor down the Lee Valley has been designated to receive up to £56 million of EU Objective 2 Structural Funds, with Stratford playing a pivotal role, including an attempt to realise the leisure and tourism potential of the huge 30 year-old Lee Valley Regional Park.

Nor are all these plans confined to the western end of the region. An awesome proposal has been put forward for developing Rainham Marshes as a Nature Conservation Theme Park, with an investment of £100 million, said to be capable of generating over one thousand direct jobs. In this climate Barking is considering a Visitor Centre for the Barking Abbey ruins and opening up Barking Creek to leisure and tourist use. The Borough of Havering has appointed a Film Locations Officer in an attempt to attract lucrative business and promote the borough to visitors at the same time.

Further cross-sectoral partnerships and sub-regional groupings have been formed to promote tourism activity. TourEast has been allocated some SRB funding for work in inner East London. To the north, the North-East London Tourism Officers Group has been formed. On a regionwide scale, recent government planning guidance envisages a revitalised River Thames with substantial leisure and transport use right out to the North Sea, with a special planning zone from Hampton Court at least as far east as the Thames Barrier.

Projected investment on this scale suggests that some powerful and appealing rationales are at play at the policy-making level.

Global rationales

The current wave of interest in tourism projects mainly derives from *global, economic factors*, which are taken to indicate *tourism's potential to contribute to urban regeneration*. The global statistics and projections are indeed impressive. For example:

- World-wide tourism has been growing at 5-6 per cent p.a. and is expected to be the largest single source of employment by the year 2000. Forecasts for the growth of UK tourism suggest a rise of 4 per cent p.a. in visitor numbers (22 million to 28 million) and a rise of 8 per cent p.a. in spending before the Millennium.
- London's global reach means that it competes primarily at international level: in 1994 London took £6.4 billion of tourism spending, an increase of 100 per cent over the last ten

years. Currently 50 per cent of all visitors to the UK arrive via London.
- London's tourist sector accounts for a direct employment total of 220,000, together with a further 150,000 indirect jobs. With the inclusion of central retailing jobs, the total grows to 500,000.
- Tourism is London's second biggest industry, after the financial and business sector, and holds the highest potential for job growth in the capital.

The East London region, of course, has a negligible share of London's massive and growing market. It is understandable if the argument prevails that an economically depressed East London simply cannot afford not to invest in an attempt to capture some of this market. Precedents for tourism development as a major focus for the regeneration of areas in severe industrial decline are not hard to find. Cities as far-flung as Barcelona, Baltimore - and within the UK - Glasgow, are sometimes cited. But before we can even begin to think through the economic and social regeneration issues of developing a tourism economy in an East London context, there are some drastic limitations, both in the realities and in the perception of them, that will have to be contended with.

Regional realities

Compare all the projected activity with the region as it currently presents itself on the ground to a sober view. Neither of the two sites with an international profile, the Tower of London and historic Greenwich, are clearly identified with the region. The Tower and its environs is after all just within the borough of Tower Hamlets, but its 2.5 million visitors are very much a part of the central London tourism economy, and appear to make little contribution to one of the poorest boroughs in the country. For all its grandeur, historic Maritime Greenwich is isolated both in transport access terms, and socially and culturally because it is hemmed in by severely deprived urban areas which make expansion difficult. The area as a whole receives less than three million visitors, which includes those counted more than once at different sites. The inner Docklands attract about a million visitors every year, about the same as Havering's country parks. At 200,000 visitors both the Horniman Museum and the Bethnal Green Museum appear heavily reliant on school parties. The Whitechapel Gallery and the Thames Barrier attract about 90,000 visitors each. And that's about it. Compare all these figures with the 20 million who flock to the Pompidou Centre alone in Paris. The rest of the East London region is hardly on anyone's map of places to visit.

There is even some evidence for concluding that the situation is getting worse rather than better. Some long-standing features such as the Passmore Edwards Museum, and more recent ventures such as the Tom Allen Arts

Top: East London skyline featuring a nineteenth-century pumping station sandwiched between the Docklands Light Railway and Canary Wharf. Bottom: Great Eastern Railway Museum at North Woolwich. Photos by Bruce Jerram.

Centre, both in Stratford, have been closed. Some new commercial attractions such as the Russian Submarine moored by the Thames Barrier Visitor Centre have recently failed. Others, such as the Great Eastern Railway Museum at North Woolwich, have never managed to get seriously established, and are constantly under threat of complete closure. And how many areas can be said to provide attractive facilities and amenities for their own residents, let alone ones worth travelling to, compared with so much that is unremarkable, or drab, or even visibly in decay? We are after all talking about a largely urban region which contains some of the most deprived populations in the whole of northern Europe.

An indication that the region as a whole currently holds virtually no attractions for visitors is the stark fact that it contains virtually no hotels suitable for them to stay in. There are truckers stops along the main arterial roads, and domestic accommodation converted into hotels, often for homeless families placed there by local councils. A clustering of small hotels to the west of the region strays into the Stoke Newington area. The three major, expensive hotels are confined to the inner Docklands area and are approaching capacity.

Moreover the lack of tourists is something which both the region's residents and those outside it take absolutely for granted, as entirely in keeping with their perceptions of the region's environmental and social defects. Visitors to the Tower and to historic Greenwich simply do not count in their perceptions of East London. In contrast to the hyperreal promise of a tourist paradise to be materialised throughout the region over the next few years, there is the pervasive assumption that East London is not plausibly, not soon, not ever, a destination for visitors. The social, economic and cultural roots of this assumption are very deeply embedded in East London's very particular history, which goes some way to explaining how this dichotomy between tourism vision and perceived reality has come about.

One Hundred Years of Solicitude

It sometimes seems as if one of East London's rare visitors must have switched off the gas lamps when he left nearly a hundred years ago. Most of the succeeding accounts of the area seem but variations on the same old story, as if no new impressions of the region could emerge with a clarity or generalised impact comparable to those of the nineteenth-century. How much is this because things really haven't changed? Or how much because social and class divisions can serve powerfully to construct and maintain our perceptions of an entire region? How much do these perceptions serve to affect and constrain our sense of the possibilities, even today?

The visitor we have in mind was Walter Besant, the year was 1899, and he recorded his impressions in his book *East London*:

> It is not a city by organisation ... It had until this year no centre, no heart ...There is no fashionable quarter; its places of amusement are of the humbler kind; there is not visible anywhere the outward indication of wealth. People, shops, houses, conveyances - all together are stamped with the unmistakable seal of the working class. Perhaps the strangest thing of all is this: in a city of two millions of people there are no hotels! That means of course there are no visitors ... There are no visitors to demand hotels; there are also none to ask for restaurants. Consequently there are none ... Is there any other city in the world, with even a tenth part of this population, of which these things could be said? (p8-10)

To turn to Besant's account is instructive, because what was seen then, at the culmination of the nineteenth-century, with a certain immediacy and perceptiveness, has so often persisted as the twentieth-century's pervasive and unquestioned assumptions. Besant was amazed that a region of London so vast and populous should have no visitors, and consequently no hotels. Yet we take it for granted that East London is still not a place to be visited, and still has virtually no hotels, after a century of some of the most rapid social change in the history of the world.

Besant goes on to link the visitor unfriendliness of East London to its industrial character:

> This crowded area, this multitude of small houses, this aggregation of mean streets - these things are the expression and the consequence of an expansion of industries on a very large and unexpected scale; East London suddenly sprang into existence because it was unexpectedly wanted ... It is a manufacturing, not a trading city; the wharves and docks are for the convenience of the merchants of the great trading city, their neighbour; they do not understand that they have any bond of common interest except the necessity of keeping order. The city sprang up so rapidly ... it has become, while men, unsuspecting went about their daily business, suddenly so vast that there has been no opportunity for the simultaneous birth or creation of any feeling of civic pride. (p8-10)

A socially-concerned chronicler with an educational mission, Besant was a precursor of probably the most persistent band of visitors yet to be attracted to East London - investigating sociologists, historians, academics, authors and journalists. For them, the labouring multitude, the urban poverty and the compensatory shifts and stratagems to which people resorted, were of positive interest. They have sought to illuminate the undifferentiated industrial murk with their candles carried for the working class and with the more powerful, if colder and narrower, electric torch-beams of theory. There is a story that the veritable searchlight of Chicago School sociology even arrived in 1925 in the form of a distinguished transatlantic professor, come to investigate what was regarded as the world's largest urban monoculture (a working class of two million). But he should have been forewarned by Besant. All the interest of sociologists has never been enough to sustain even one hotel. Finding no university in East London to study in, and no hotel to stay in, the distinguished professor left. We shall never know if he would have brought new perspectives, but it is striking, if understandable, that Besant's successors have continued to define East London almost entirely in terms of what it lacks. A recent contribution to the genre was a series of articles in the *Evening Standard* entitled 'London Betrayed'.

Where does it get us, to read Besant, when we live and work in East London at the end of the twentieth-century? We might note that in a sense we still do not know where we are at all, in terms of the region as a whole - no civic focus has yet evolved commensurate with the region's scale. We might link this amorphousness in the social geography of the region with the continuing lack of visitors. We must above all note a fundamental change:

the economy of factories and docks which generated East London has collapsed over the last thirty years.

And so the solicitude intensifies, as the deficiences are listed. But if we attend with Besant's questioning sense of surprise to both what has changed as well as to what has not, we can at least see where the positive tourism scenario arises. Might not the collapse of smokestack industries and their attendant environments, which previously rendered East London either repellent or uninteresting to visit, and which continue to do so when left in a derelict state, at least potentially open up East London to visitors? Optimism increases as further changes are taken into account which begin to hold out the prospect of East London again surprising the world: this time by bringing an end to over one hundred years of solicitude through triumphantly overcoming its unrelieved history of solitude.

Developing infrastructures, realising assets

Several factors now favour the breakdown of the historic economic, social and cultural divide which has hitherto segregated East London from the rest of the City. In an intensely competitive global market it is only on a regional basis that any area can hope to sustain itself. Just as East London needs to become integrated into the tourism economies of central, west, and to some extent north, London, the World City needs East London (just as it needed it as a site of industrial production and port activities in the last century, but effectively denied the connection, as Besant acutely noted). The traditional central sites suffer from overheating, including a chronic shortage of hotel accommodation. There is some recognition at the level of London Tourist Board policy of the need to draw tourists to boroughs beyond Westminster and the central zone. Moreover, London's share of the world tourism market is far from assured, even if the overall growth of the sector in London is maintained - the city badly needs new attractions and a fresh impetus if it is to remain competitive. The tourism legacy of the Millennium Exhibition site in East London is probably London's best chance of receiving such a boost, as well as of establishing East London on the national and international map of tourism destinations for good.

Decisively, the transport infrastructure is now being put in place, to make such integration between the economies of the east and the rest of London a practical reality. The Jubilee Line Extension (JLE) and the Docklands Light Railway (DLR) should make all the difference. And on a regional and international basis, recent developments and decisions mean that East London itself will enjoy major new advantages into the next century. The international rail terminal for the Channel Tunnel recently awarded to Stratford is the most significant of these. It will encourage tourism flows to disperse down to Docklands and across the river to the south side of the Thames as well as eastwards to the outer areas of the Gateway. London City Airport provides even quicker access to Europe, and could grow to play a more prominent role. East London is very well placed to draw in overseas visitors directly from Stansted, the fastest growing airport in Europe. The trunk road system in the region has been recently much improved, and if the new river crossing ever materialises this will be a very significant event. The local road traffic system within East London remains a nightmare, but then in our view it is public transport which must surely become the means of the future. The Woolwich Rail Crossing will provide the North London Line with a link to the entire South Eastern commuter and putative tourist system.

Equally crucial to the development of East London tourism is the availability of prime river and waterside sites, consequent upon the closure of the docks and the almost total release of the Thames in East London from the industrial uses which dominated the scene until the last few decades. The value of such sites has initially been materialised in terms of commercial office property speculation, through the billions of investment in the Canary Wharf development, supported by the

London Docklands Development Corporation (LDDC). However poor a model this development provides for urban regeneration which is sensitive to the needs and interests of local populations, and therefore for the type of tourism development we will be going on to discuss, there are some important lessons to be learnt. One is that the spectacular architecture, waterside ambience and retail and catering provision have generated a largely unintended tourism dimension to the area, especially via the overground DLR. The LDDC is now taking tourism more into account as part of its exit strategy. Another is that without an adequate transport infrastructure in place, such major new developments of any kind will fail - the whole complex has only been saved from ruin by the Government's belated implementation of the JLE link. As it is, Canary Wharf has done East London at least some service by giving the inner docks area an unmistakable public profile, and promoting an eastward shift in London's whole centre of gravity. Tourism-led urban regeneration elsewhere in the UK and abroad, such as in the cities already referred to, has very often focused on former port, dockland and riverside sites. East London does not just provide probably the biggest redevelopment site in Europe, the River Thames and the Lee ensure locations of prime topographical value. The list of tourism projects and proposals for East London, above, very much takes the form of extending visitor attractions eastwards down the Thames and along the Lee. Access to the riverbank and the use of riverboats for transport and leisure is at last receiving the attention it deserves, and the outcome will be one of the single most important factors in establishing East London as a sustainable tourism economy. But the marked tendency to extend consideration no further east than the Thames Barrier must be overcome. A helpful factor here is that it is not just industrial sites which are becoming available down the river. The peace dividend and privatisation is leading to the release of a significant amount of Ministry of Defence Thames-side land, such as the sites for the Woolwich Arsenal and Rainham Marshes proposals.

Yet if global economic developments, regional infrastructural improvements, and the availability of prime sites are all underlying the drive for tourism development, the type, the processes and the implications of such development in an East London context do still require careful thought.

Waving, not drowning

At times the undiscriminating enthusiasm for tourism development, based on tourism's economic importance, can sound like a merely fashionable counsel of despair for blighted, formerly industrial areas, where all else is visibly failing- its advocates but blinkered devotees of the 'Marie Antoinette' school of urban regeneration: 'Madame, the people lack employment, their neighbourhoods are impoverished and decaying'. 'Then let them have tourism'.

For one thing, global statistics do not differentiate between desirable and exploitative relationships. Concerns about the 'sex tourism' industries in Thailand, most recently focusing on child prostitution, provide an extreme example. Given the continuing class and power inequalities, and the often disastrous twentieth-century record of East London being more planned against than planning, we do need to be wary. The tourism-led economy may boom, but who benefits and who gets the money? Recent TV documentary publicity about the devious and exploitative employment practices of some of London's major multinational hotels should alert us to the importance of such issues, should this be in any doubt. Could the tourism-led regeneration dream be but a gloss for preparing an impoverished, unskilled and unproductive East London population for an economy of last resort, because they have nothing to sell but their culture, their history, their identity, the best of their natural environment, and their own menial services? Without a strong political and civic focus, East London may be particularly vulnerable to the social costs of tourism development, as it was to those of industrialisation. What we want to avoid is a glossy tourism economy superimposed on a region whose inhabitants will be left merely as impoverished onlookers, doormen, or chambermaids, for visitors moving only between a few carefully circumscribed prime sites.

The key to benign development surely lies in the extent to which the interests and activities of residents are represented and taken into account through the available range of partnership and consultation processes. The democratisation of the tourist experience itself over the last few decades is of particular value here. To the extent that we are almost all tourists now, what is good for tourists is or should be good for residents, and vice-versa. Today's tourism, even in East London's potentially global context, is very far from being confined to the activities of stereotypically camera-toting, rich foreigners. Tourism is often but one, travel-related dimension, of social activities which are being pursued for a variety of purposes: visits to friends and relatives, religious observance, conference and business trips as well as holidays. It can be defined in terms of visitor-usage of a number of associated sectors, notably: hotels and catering; commercial visitor attractions and cultural and heritage facilities; sporting facilities and clubs; and retailing.

The importance of improving amenities and facilities for East London's residents as a basis for attracting visitors can hardly be over-emphasised. Visitors need to feel comfortable enough with their surroundings, as well as being attracted to specific facilities. Crime or environmental blight affect them as well as residents. This is particularly important for East London, because our audit of sites with visitor potential suggests that the region does in fact have quite as rich a texture of sightseeing attractions, of live entertainment, and of leisure activities to offer as West London. What is lacking is investment in, and marketing of, these features - and this is problematic because the 'bits-in-between' are often too blighted to allow the crucial clusters of varied amenities and facilities to coalesce into an attractive area. Walthamstow, for example, has a museum of international significance in the William Morris Gallery, and other sites which occur no-where else in the capital, such as an eighteenth-century vestry house and a nineteenth-century police-station, complete with cells. There is an integrated historic site Walthamstow Village, with attendant consumer outlets; trattoria, pubs, art and bric-a-brac shops. It boasts the longest street market in Europe, and a variety of nightlife experiences from the Forest Theatre to London's largest dog-racing stadium. Even the 1930s Town Hall is of architectural interest (All this is readily accessible by rail, road and tube - just seventeen minutes from the centre of London. Beyond this centre lie some of the greatest expanses of preserved water and greenery around the Metropolis, and a further sprinkling of historic buildings such as Queen Elizabeth's Hunting Lodge on the edge of Epping Forest. Given some local environmental improvements, signage to link attractions together, and some intelligent marketing, the 'critical mass' surely exists for a positive and prolonged tourist experience, attracting a very wide range of visitors, local, regional and international.

Such area-based developments would ideally complement the more spectacular proposed attractions and travel infrastructure nodes. Indeed there is a strong case for saying that new flagship attractions should be related as closely as possible to the distinctive history, culture and environment of the region. In an age when the latest fashion in lookalike attractions can be rapidly built, and copied and trumped, in any corner of the country or the world, the sustainability of an attraction is likely to depend at least partly on its distinctiveness, and on a local sense of participation, commitment and ownership. For example, a historic-ship based Museum of the Merchant Marine, with related river-going activities and maintenance trades, would provide such an attraction of this kind for the Royal Docks. Or in terms of a distinctive travel experience, investing to improve the North London Line as an orbital

Two aspects of Walthamstow: top, sixteenth-century Walthamstow village. Bottom, Walthamstow Town Hall, built 1933. Photos by Bruce Jerram.

overground tourism route, linking established attractions in the west and north of London with new ones in the east, would at the same time improve environmentally sustainable transport facilities for local residents.

A tourism-development approach for the region must also be based on its residents' existing strengths, as well as on the assets of its localities. East London has some particular traditional strengths, for example in the areas of the visual and performing arts, design, fashion, and fabrics. The British Tourist Authority is emphasising precisely these elements in its current UK marketing campaign to overseas visitors, especially the youth sector. East London could have much to contribute to strengthening and profiting by 'Britain's image as a stylish, contemporary and vibrant destination', including the contributions of the region's significant ethnic minority populations. Fashion and popular music influenced by the Indian sub-continent, for example, is currently enjoying a national vogue.

As already indicated, the provision of visitor accommodation is fundamental to developing the region's tourism economy: it is above all through hotels that income is generated from tourism. There are some signs that commercial investment is just beginning. Not far from the empty Galleons Reach hotel, mothballed by the LDDC, is the always-full new Travel Inn, sited near the headstop of the DLR at Beckton. The latest of the region's hotel developments is the 'Formule 1' on the North Circular at Barking. This concept is the product of the French conglomerate ARRO, which opened its first unit in 1991, and aims to have 1,000 hotels across Europe by the year 2000. Key to the success of this no-fuss basic, modular, and very cheap accommodation is a huge 2.5 per cent of turnover investment in staff training, which puts the UK hospitality industry's record of personnel investment to shame. The scope for East London to offer hospitality at the cheaper end of the market, including the camping and caravanning sectors, with rapid access to central London and to its own attractions, is immense. As an international transport node, Stratford is set to join the big hotel league. One problem with the Thames Gateway concept is that people don't tend to stop at a gateway, however major, they tend to go through it. The East London region must be persuasively marketed at such nodes to ensure at least some of the visitors explore the area as well as heading off for the centre or out to Europe.

Above all, it is investment in training and education on a region-wide basis that will be the most crucial factor in enabling the regional labour market to take proper advantage of the new opportunities. Vocational training in tourism-related crafts and skills is notoriously deficient in terms of both quality and quantity in this country,

Top: Not a hotel, Galleons Reach, fully renovated and empty in the outer docks.
Bottom: Not a museum, HQ of a local urban regeneration agency. Photos by Bruce Jerram.

but this only increases the need for regional providers such as the TECs to take a lead. UEL's investigations also suggest that educational provision at management and strategic planning level is if anything of even greater urgency. The university is therefore pioneering some short-course post-experience provision for the region, which may well develop into establishing postgraduate vocational degrees in such specialisms as urban tourism.

Of course some conflicts of interest will inevitably arise. Current examples at the local level include the growing impatience among Whitechapel residents at their neighbourhood being marketed as the scene of Jack the Ripper's crimes, and anxieties in Hackney at the promotion of a 'twenty-four hour' leisure economy. But these kinds of inconvenience can often be sensibly resolved and become relatively insignificant when compared with the economic, social and cultural benefits which a visitor economy could bring.

Could bring, that is, as long as the interests and needs of the region's residents are fully represented and provided for as part of the process. Only then will a successful visitor economy lessen rather than exacerbate social exclusion and isolation. In that case the signals coming out of East London will no longer be perceived as those of the drowning appealing for rescue, but as the welcoming wave of the swimmer which says 'having a wonderful time, come on in'. At that point private investment of all kinds as well as public investment will truly begin to pour into the region.

And at that point the region worth visiting will also have become a place in which even the most skilled and successful daughters and sons of East London will wish to stay put.

The Art of Cable Street

Roger Mills

When the police came down on horses, you see, we thought that Mosley was going to march after them, but they didn't. People were throwing bedding, tables, chairs, everything out of the window to build the barricades. It was terrific to watch. Something you could never forget. I can remember the old girls with their aprons on and the mens caps that they used to wear in those days with shawls round their shoulders and glory on their faces. I'd like to be able to do a picture.[1]

Somebody *did* eventually do a picture. A giant mural of the Battle was painted on the west wall of St George's Town Hall in Cable Street itself. It's still there and provided a focal point for some of the commemorative events which took place over the last few months of 1996, the sixtieth anniversary of the Battle of Cable Street.

Although it is the primary purpose

of this article to look at the various ways that painters, playwrights and other artists have used and interpreted the events of October 4th 1936, and the period leading up to it, it is worth looking first at the story of the actual battle.

By 1936, both Italy and Germany were ruled by fascist regimes. Also in that year, civil war had broken out in Spain between the Republican Government and fascist rebels. In Britain, Sir Oswald Mosley, who had previously been a member of both the Conservative Party and the Labour Party, attempted to emulate what he saw as a successful and growing international movement, setting up his own British Union of Fascists (BUF). Taking note of the tactics and supposed appeal of his continental models, the BUF was injected with a large dose of anti-semitism.

In the East End of London, the area with the largest Jewish population in Britain, meetings were held to discuss the threat posed by the BUF's anti-semitic propaganda and the increasing number of physical attacks by Mosley's 'blackshirts'. The announcement that the BUF were to stage a huge march through the area on October 4th was seen as an escalation of the BUF's activities and, as Battle veteran William J. Fishman records, 'an act of provocation, ostensibly aimed at the dual targets of Fascist attack: Jews and Communists'.[2] In response to the BUF's plans, the Jewish Peoples Council organised a petition calling on the march to be stopped. The petition was signed by 100,000 people, but even with the support of local Labour MP George Lansbury and the mayors of the four East London boroughs, the Home Secretary, Sir John Simon, refused to consider a ban.

The people of the East End and political activists were in disarray. Labour leaders, the Board of Deputies of British Jews and The *Daily Herald* all urged the local population to simply ignore it. And, initially, the Communist Party called on members to stay away because the date clashed with a Young Communist League rally - in support of the Spanish Republicans - which had already been arranged to take place in Trafalgar Square. A fudge was proposed but, as Joe Jacobs recorded, tensions were mounting:

> We in the Communist Party were supposed to tell people to go to Trafalgar Square and come back in the evening to protest after Mosley had marched...How could they be so blind to what was happening in Stepney? The slogan 'They Shall Not Pass' was already on everyone's lips and being whitewashed on walls and pavements.[3]

Eventually, due to pressure from local activists, the Communist Party leadership relented and on October 2nd, the *Daily Worker* declared 'East End rallies against Fascism...Youth Meet transferred'. The Spanish Republicans' defiant words 'They Shall

Not Pass' were officially adopted, although there was now precious little time to draw up plans to halt the march. Also preparing for the day were, amongst others, the Independent Labour Party, the Jewish Ex-Serviceman's Association and local men and women, Jew and Gentile, not aligned to any particular grouping at all.

Because the route that Mosley's blackshirts intended to take was not clear, his opponents gathered in four key points of entry to the area, Gardiners Corner in Aldgate, Leman Street, St George's Street (now the Highway) and Cable Street, with fights breaking out as the blackshirts approached. The main battle however was between the estimated 250,000 anti-fascists (some put the figure even higher) and the 6000 police, including the entire mounted division, who had been drafted in to clear a path for the march. Baton charges were made but at Gardiners Corner a tram was immobilised, ruling it out as a possible way in to the area. Because of difficulties in using any of the other points, it became clear that the route Mosley would use to gain access would be through Cable Street.

Once again, the resourcefulness of the anti-fascists had been underestimated. When an overturned lorry was brought into play as a barrier to the police and blackshirts, a fierce battle ensued. Joyce Goodman recalls:

There were people going straight through the plate glass windows. There were horses coming straight into the crowd, and the police were just hitting anyone indis-criminately. We never saw a fascist all that day. We were fighting the police. They were just hitting everyone, there were women going down under the horses' hooves. Absolute terror.[4]

Arrests and injuries were inevitable. When it became obvious to all that the march would not be able to proceed, the Metropolitan Police Com-missioner, Sir Phillip Game, finally gave the order that Mosley would have to abandon his attempted affront to the people of East London. William J. Fishman has written of its finish - and of a beginning.

By late afternoon, the Fascist 'army' was forced to turn about and march off in the opposite direction: through the deserted City, along the Embankment, where, in the absence of an audience, they quickly dispersed. That night there was dancing in the pubs and in the side streets of the East End. And thus was a legend born.[5]

All the anti-fascists present on the day knew that by their efforts they had written themselves into the history books. Not surprisingly, the occasion has become an emblem for the British left, particularly for those involved in struggles where physical confrontation has played a part. What is surprising however, given the different factions and groupings involved, is just how little disagreement there is about interpretation of the facts surrounding the event. It is my opinion that, in part, it is this untroubled recollection that smoothed the way when a mural depicting the Battle was proposed. It had been, just about everybody agreed, a resounding success in the fight against British fascism.

In 1976, the Tower Hamlets Arts Project, a community organisation formed in that year, looked at proposals for the mural artwork. The ensuing process is described here.

> Dave Binnington and Desmond Rochford of the Public Arts Workshop were chosen to carry out the work. Binnington, who had studied the murals of Siquieros and Rivera, conducted intense historical research. He looked at books, films and photographs of the event and worked much of what he found into his design: the dramatic uniforms of the BUF, the eggs, milk bottles, tools and the contents of chamber-pots coming from the upper windows, the mounted police 'Cossacks' with long weighted clubs surging through the crowd, the use of marbles and ball bearings against the police horses, the overturned lorry, the chairs and mattresses of the barricade and the police autogyro flying overhead. Binnington interviewed and drew many local characters, including them in the design which was made into a slide, projected on to the wall and carefully drawn in.[6]

It was perhaps inevitable that the mural would attract the attention of supporters of far-right political groups which had become increasingly active in Tower Hamlets during the 1970s. Work on the mural was well underway when, in 1982, the scaffold which the artist was using to carry out the ongoing work acted as the device by which fascists were able to deface it with anti-left and racist graffiti. The bold six-foot high letters in white paint caused massive damage.

The mural was finally completed in 1983, when after the departure of Dave Binnington, Desmond Rochford worked with artists Paul Butler and Ray Walker. This phase of the work saw modifications and emphasis in the design. The concept of featuring contemporary inhabitants of Cable Street was retained however. Black and Asian faces were featured and although it is unlikely that it is this radical feature of the mural alone that sent fascists scurrying out with spraypaint and brushes in the dead of night (the mural has suffered other, more minor, attacks in the intervening years), it emphasised the modern parallel situation where people from these groups had supplanted Jews as the main object of fascist aggression. By the way, this last statement is not meant to indicate a belief on my part that the mural purposely sets out to misrepresent and that none of the anti-fascists were black. Rather, as far as I am aware, that their presence had not been featured in representations until that point.

Sketch for the Cable Street Mural 1982, Ray Walker

Desmond Rochford, in writing about Ray Walker after his death at the tragically young age of thirty-nine, emphasised the joint nature of their work together on the mural.

> ...the experience of collaborating aesthetically and politically, to redesign and complete this huge mural proved as much an inspiration to Ray as it did to myself and Paul Butler. The necessary aesthetic and imaginative compromises that are at the heart of all the great collaborative arts, such as theatre and the cinema, do not diminish ideas and imagination. Rather they enchance and strengthen them, particularly when aims and intentions are not in dispute.[7]

The Battle has, apart from in historical texts and autobiography, been recorded in drama more than in any other art form. It's hard to believe that the story hasn't already been made into a feature film (there are rumours of an as yet unproduced film script still lying in the bottom drawer of a well-known television writer), but it has provided the basis for several theatre productions.

Unlike the Cable Street Mural, which is able to represent the furious images of the battle itself, stagebound works have traditionally been saddled with a realist setting, telling, mostly in dialogue, of the events leading up to October the 4th, with characters running on and off stage and only being able to *describe* the turmoil that they are unable to show us. In October 1996, the Light 'n' Shade Theatre Company performed *The Battle of Cable Street* by Simon Blumenfeld at the Hackney Empire Studio Theatre. Simon Blumenfeld, still writing today, has the distinction of having been a bestselling author even before the battle. His novels *Jew Boy*, (1935) and *Phineas Kahn* (1937) chart the lives of characters in the Jewish community, both immigrant and English-born. His Cable Street play, previously performed at the Edinburgh Festival in 1987, begins with a prologue mapping out the political scene of the 1930s, moving from there to scenes, set mostly in a cafe, where the characters lead us through the story in a clear chronological order. Apart from the cafe proprietor and his wife there is a young male firebrand and female student - who are involved in a romance - and a number of other characters representing the differing attitudes towards Mosley's threat. Initial Communist Party prevarication on the national level and community frustration are represented, as are local workers in the shape of an elderly Jewish tailor and supporters such as an Irish docker. One of the young activists is played by a black actor and the play succesfully conjours up the spirit, if not the images, described by Charlie Goodman.

> ...it was not just a question of Jews being there on 4th October, the most amazing thing was to see a

silk-coated Orthodox Jew standing next to an Irish docker with a grappling iron. This was absolutely unbelievable. Because it is not a question of...a punch-up between the Jews and fascists, it was a question of the people who understood what fascism was.'[8]

The Battle also featured in the play *No Pasaran* by David Holman, written while he worked with the M6 Theatre Company in Bolton in the 1970s. This version followed the fictional journey of a young Jewish boxer who witnesses first-hand the rise of fascism in Germany, who on travelling to England, sees it's shadow fall over East London. The Battle was used, perhaps most famously, in the first act of *Chicken Soup with Barley*, written by Arnold Wesker and first performed in 1958. This was the first of a trilogy by Wesker featuring the character Ronnie Kahn, the other two plays being *Roots* and *I'm talking about Jerusalem*. Wesker's father was a refugee from Russia, his mother from Hungary. Born in the East End in 1932, he would have grown up with the legend of the Battle resounding in his ears. Here, the playwright, as in the other versions, becomes a self-appointed 'community historian', weaving details of the day into the drama. The following dialogue from *Chicken Soup with Barley* sets out to illustrate the careful planning that had taken place prior to the Battle.

DAVE. Take your pick, Sarah. If you fancy yourself as a nurse then go to Aldgate, we've got a first-aid post there, near Whitechapel Library.
SARAH. Such organization! And you lot?
DAVE. Monty is taking some of the lads to the left flank of Cable Street, Prince is organizing a team of cyclist messengers between the main points and headquarters, I'm going round the streets at the last minute to call everyone out - and that's the lot.
MONTY. (rubbing his hands). All we have to do is wait.[9]

But, of course, we the audience don't get to leave the kitchen. It was with the limitations of stage work in mind that the community-based WOOF Theatre Company, approached the subject in a very different way. Their show, *Shattersongs,* by Alan Gilbey was performed in East London's Half Moon Theatre in the late 1980s. This used cabaret-style songs, comedy and striking, semi-surreal images to show not just the Battle of 1936 but to also encompass contemporary anti-fascist activity. The production presented a much less triumphal view of the battle. At one stage a character steps out of a frozen human tableau to question his role in a heroic propaganda poster. And in one of the songs, 'The Art of Glazing', the point is made that perhaps fascism in all its forms will *never* be fully defeated and that constant vigilance and resistance is essential. Hardly the usual stuff of agitprop, yet the script's constant fast-forwarding to the present day, hammers home the relevance of the event for an audience of today.

Shattersongs was based on an earlier, more small-scale production by the group, *You Should Have Been There*, a one-hour promenade performance. Again, using bold verbal and visual statements rather than an adherance to accepted historical facts. The image of an actor playing the ghost of Oswald Mosley, stomping around the Old Synagogue in Princlet Street, Spitalfields, where it was staged, was a provocative one.

The event has been recorded in poetry by, amongst others, the 'Tramp Poet', an East End ex-serviceman who had lost a leg and an arm. He wrote broadsheet poems and sold them in Oxford Street. His poem, 'The Battle of Cable Street' has been reproduced in various collections including *Bricklight - an anthology of poetry from the labour movement in East London*, edited in 1980 by teacher Chris Searle. Performance poet Leah Thorn also wrote several pieces for use in sessions with young children. As part of the sixtieth anniversary commemorations, Eastside (formerly the Tower Hamlets Arts Project), arranged for her to work in primary schools in or near Cable Street itself. The children's work deriving from these sessions was later exhibited at a commemorative event.

In all the examples given so far, the writers and painters, even if they were not present on the day, would have had access to written accounts of the period on which to base their work. The Battle of Cable Street looms large in two autobiographies, *Out of the Ghetto: My Youth in the East End. Communism and Fascism 1919-1939* (1978) by Joe Jacobs, and *Our Flag Stays Red* (1948) by Phil Piratin. It also plays a more minor part in others. There is a vivid account of the Battle in Jim Wolveridge's book *Ain't it Grand: or This was Stepney*.

> The woman who owned the fruit shop had neglected to put up her shutters and the crowd pinched her fruit to throw at the police. She didn't like it much but it was all in a good cause. One of the crowd threw a large pair of pliers at a policeman, but it missed him and went through my guvnor's basement window. Old Feldman paid such lousy wages I'd often felt like throwing things through his window myself, but it was a pity it missed the copper.'[9]

The flight of the pliers is a good example of how such sources have provided images for artists. The image was incorporated directly into the Cable Street Mural. Even as I write, I note that the Battle has been used as background material in a new novel in the 'family-saga' genre. *All Shadows Fly Away* by Audrey Willshire acknowledges in the introduction the assistance of Battle veterans Charlie and Joyce Goodman.

There have been various first-hand accounts by Charlie Goodman and others in their own right, as well as accounts by historians such as William

J. Fishman, who was also there on the day. It has featured in television documentaries and in a booklet, *The Battle of Cable Street 1936*, primarily aimed at secondary school students. This last publication was compiled by The Cable Street Group, formed by some of the people who had been involved in the fiftieth anniversay march ten years ago. Its members have strong associations with the street, either through work or because they live there or nearby. Their aim is to produce information about the culture of the area from the turn of the century to the present day. To this end, they have conducted interviews with many, mainly older inhabitants of the street, most of who have now moved away. The Battle was just one aspect of their lives that they spoke about. Edited transcripts of the interviews are featured in the booklet. The group also organised one of this year's sixtieth anniversary events and were behind the campaign several years ago to save the Cable Street Mural when building work at the Town Hall threatened to deface it. Its defence was supported by playwright Steven Berkoff amongst others.

Other artifacts surrounding the Battle include a sixtieth anniversary plate, produced by a group of ex-miners; a 'trade union style' banner incorporating the languages of the modern East End and used on various marches; postcards and posters featuring aspects of the mural and a badge, produced in 1986 during the Wapping dispute between newspaper magnate Rupert Murdoch and the print unions. The badge was not intended to draw an exact parallel between the nature of the two events but as a reminder that people sometimes have no alternative but to take to the streets. In the case of the Wapping dispute, as pickets. The memory of the Battle was also invoked during the late 1980s for a series of anti-racist concerts. 'Cable Street Beat' was formed to counter the rise of performances by rock groups allied to extreme right-wing organisations. With its own logo and slogan 'Music Against Fascism' Cable Street Beat staged events featuring groups such as The Men They Couldn't Hang, The Neurotics and poetry 'ranter' Attila the Stockbroker.

Sixty years and still going strong. If anything, the Battle of Cable Street seems to be growing as a memory to rally round, as an event to be commemorated in word and image and song. Perhaps one day that film will happen, its stars appearing on TV chat shows and talking to an even larger audience about the day the people of the East End took on the high-born Oswald Mosley, the fascists, the police - and won. There will almost certainly be a seventieth anniversary commemoration in ten years time and I suspect that there will also be a hundreth anniversary event in 2036, by which time of course there will be no veterans left to remember it. But

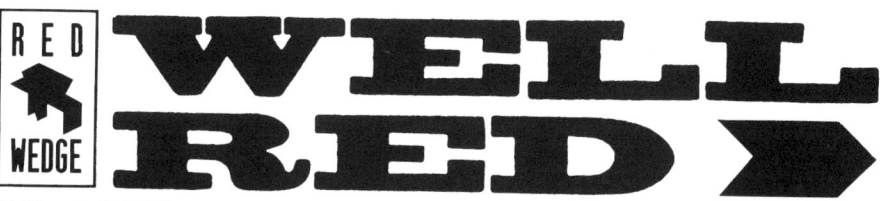

A Quarterly POP and POLITICS Magazine from RED WEDGE ✳ No. 7   70 PENCE

centres.

Mike Figgis' **STORMY MONDAY** is the best so far. Set in Newcastle, it's inner city decay and towering redundant dockyards are transformed by cinematographer Roger Deakins into a seamy neon-lit world of bars and clubs that would do justice to downtown Chicago.

One such, a jazz club, is the centre of the film. It is here that Sting, playing the seedy owner, Finney, is holding out in the last property on the block not to be sold to American property speculator David Cosmo (played frighteningly by Tommy Lee Jones). It is here that young drifter Brendan (Sean Bean) quickly gets involved with both Finney and Melanie Griffith's Kate, an American waitress who, unbeknownst to him, is on Cosmo's payroll. The situation escalates into a fraught and violent thriller played out to the tune of the marching bands that accompany America Week – a celebration of Anglo-American friendship – and to the sound of jazz, particularly the avant garde variety provided hilariously by the Krakow Jazz Ensemble, in town to play Finney's club.

It is a film deep with irony, resplendent with talent – Griffith playing a remarkably restrained role and Sting breaking his duck by actually acting in this one – and awash with a black humour that is tempered by Figgis' obvious feel for and elequent use of the music that is such a powerful factor in this multi-layered emotional masterpiece. ▼ Chris Collins

NO RIGHT TURN

In 1936 Cable Street in East London was the scene of a famous fiercely fought victory when 250,000 anti-fascists stopped Sir Oswald Mosley's Blackshirts from marching through a Jewish working class area. Cable Street Beat is a new organisation launched this summer to take the anti-fascist message, through music, to a new audience to mobilise support for demos, pickets and meetings. Although the NF and BM now rarely hold demos or stand in elections, there are 70,000 racist attacks a year and there's a growing nazi youth culture. Cable Street Beat believe it is vital to establish a militant anti-fascist tradition in popular youth culture, so are asking for support from bands, promoters, DJs – anyone who is willing to help organise, design banners or, more critically, raise money. Contact them at PO BOX 273, Forest Gate, London E7. ▼ Hilary Cross

DEVIL WORSHIP

It's official – working for the Tory press rots your brains. After a couple of years scribbling cynical columns for the *Mail On Sunday*, former enfant terrible and self-professed Communist Julie Burchill has finally done the decent thing and come out in full public support of Margaret Thatcher. Looking back on the Eighties in issue 100 of *The Face*, the Stalinist yuppie hails Thatcher for "making Britain great again", somehow managing to overlook our role as lame poodle to Reagan's USA. *Well Red* is sure that the Libyan children bombed by British-based US aircraft, the pensioners who fought in the last war who have had their pensions cut, and the 80,000 registered homeless young Britons will all agree with the one-time punk rocker that Britain is once more great. ▼ [illegible]

ISSUE 7 • **WELL RED**

Cable Street beat, from Well Red, *September 1988*

their story and their words have been recorded for posterity and if the underlying message of *Shattersongs* is true - that fascism in some shape or form will always be with us - then there will be artists for generations to come who will draw on the Battle of Cable Street's power for their inspiration.

> Remember those who stood up for
> Their daughters and their sons
> Listen to the sound of marching feet
> And the voices of the ghosts of Cable Street
> Fists, stones, batons and the gun
> With courage we shall beat those Blackshirts down.[11]

REFERENCES

1. Gershon, J., in *The Battle of Cable Street 1936*, The Cable Street Group, London 1995.

2. Fishman, W. J., 'A People's Journee: The Battle of Cable Street', (October 4th 1936) in Frederick Krantz (ed), *History from Below: Studies in Popular Ideology in Honour of George Rude*, Concordia University, Montreal 1985.

3. Jacobs, J., *Out of the Ghetto: My Youth in the East End. Communism and Fascism 1919-1939*, Janet Simon, London 1978, Reprinted Phoenix Press 1991.

4. Goodman, J., in P. Catterall (ed), 'The Battle of Cable Street revisited', *Contemporary Record*, Volume 8, Number1, Summer 1994, Frank Cass, London.

5. Fishman, *op. cit.*

6. *The Battle of Cable Street 1936*, The Cable Street Group, London.

7. Rochford, D., in *Ray Walker*, The Ray Walker Memorial Committee (ed), Coracle Press, London 1985.

8. Goodman, C., in P. Catteral, *op. cit.*, 1994.

9. Wesker, A.., *The Wesker Trilogy*, Longmans, London 1968.

10. Wolveridge, J., *Ain't it Grand: or This was Stepney*, Stepney Books London 1976.

11. 'Ghosts of Cable Street', on *How Green is the Valley*, Men They Couldn't Hang, MCA Records, London 1986.

REVIEWS

A Good Death
Michael Young & Lesley Cullen
Routledge, 1996. £13.99.

Carole Satyamurti

In a society where we do all we can to avoid contemplating mortality, 'a good death' may seem like a contradiction in terms. When we hear of someone dying unexpectedly in their sleep, we tend to feel that such a death is to be envied - the kind of death we would wish for ourselves when the time comes, the kind you don't see coming, so have no time to dread. By that reckoning, the only good death would be one of which one is unaware - good, by virtue of its absence from consciousness.

It would follow that the people whose deaths are described in this book must have had very bad deaths indeed. Young and Cullen followed the lives of fourteen terminally ill people, all dying of cancer, from the point of initial contact until they died. These were slow deaths, ones which, typically, followed a trajectory from the bad news about their condition, via a succession of treatments, remissions, deteriorations and further treatments, to the point where palliative care was all that remained. Emotionally, this was a switchback composed of shock, disbelief, despair, hope, disappointment, denial, anger, resignation. No individual experienced all of these, nor necessarily in this order, but painful emotions were acknowledged to be an integral part of the experience of nearly all the informants. Yet Young and Cullen succeed in convincing us, through the material they present, that many of their informants did have a good death.

Most of the informants were obtained via St Joseph's Hospice in Hackney - one of the oldest hospices in the country (founded in 1905) and a major East End institution. They were all people who, in the opinion of their doctors, had between three and four months to live. The researchers visited each person as often as was convenient for that person and, after their death, continued to visit the carer, when allowed, for up to a year. (The number of visits ranged from three to thirty-eight).

It was agreed with the hospice that the researchers would not say anything about the prognosis, and they could not, therefore, ask direct questions about death. However, this constraint on the research design seems not to have been an obstacle to gleaning a full picture of how each person was facing the end. The fact that the majority were patients of the hospice (though most were being cared for at home, with Home Support Services) must have meant that they were aware that their doctors regarded them as being terminally ill. Most people spoke freely, albeit sometimes indirectly, about their impending deaths. It seems likely that, had the informants been obtained through GPs, the picture would have been different.

As would be expected from other studies, with few exceptions, the main carers tended to be wives and daughters. The way that family members rallied round, even those living at some distance and with their own busy lives, was not, perhaps, surprising. More striking was the extent to which neighbours and friends stepped in, for people who had no family, taking on a nursing and caring role in relation to the patient to a quite astonishing extent. A sudden death is devastating for those left, but a slow dying process can place an enormous strain on carers, and the authors show the relationship between the time scale of the dying process and what carers, even with support, can manage.

Hospitals show up badly in this account. It is clear that doctors can often be insensitive at best, and callous at worst in their management of these patients who are not going to get better. Working-class patients are sometimes treated by middle-class doctors as though they were stupid and of no account. GPs, working with patients in the community, are more responsive to their needs.

A good death has various dimensions, but all of them have to do with the possibility of a person being able to retain their personhood until the end. For this, they should obviously not be in the kind of pain that makes it impossible for them to attend to anything else. Most of these informants, cared for by the hospice team, had their pain under control most of the time. Many were in control of their own pain relief, highlighting another aspect of personhood - a sense of autonomy. Some recounted experiences of being in hospital, at an earlier stage in their illness, where they were often made to feel dehumanised, and had no say in what happened to them, or when. At home, or in the Hospice, they often chose to experience *some* pain, deriving psychological benefit from the sense of managing it, and of having a choice. As Julia said, 'you need pain so you are aware you are alive' (p132). To be an agent in one's life, rather than the passive recipient of medical procedures, was important to most, though not all, the informants. Research has indicated that a person who feels they have some control over their illness and its management tends to survive longer, and the longest survivors in this study exemplify this.

The ability to incorporate the new fact of imminent death into an already meaningful life was a key to many people's possibility of dying a good death. For the older participants in the study, this tended to be easier than for the younger ones. Sometimes aided by a belief in an afterlife, where they would encounter their dead relatives, they were able to feel that their death was natural. Even without religious belief, there is a sense that, for older people, death comes as less of an affront - an exception being Dora, who had recently formed an attachment to a man friend, and who was resentful about the fact that she was dying.

Dying is intensely personal and, at the same time, socially mediated. The most important ingredient in a meaningful life, for many of the informants, was the existence of strong family relationships in which the person played a role that could be sustained, despite their illness. Although the East End is in many ways a different place from that described by Young and Willmott nearly forty years ago (Young and Willmott, 1957) many were embedded in families in which people saw each other several times a week. Kenneth, one of the three who defied for longest the doctors' predictions, remained, to the end, the head of his large family, asked for his advice, and regularly visited by his four daughters and their children. In other cases, family members who had not been in frequent contact became closer after the diagnosis.

Much of this would suggest that a prerequisite of a good death is a good life, but this would be a misleading assumption. One of the most moving accounts in the book is of Dermot, an isolated Irish manual worker who found in the Hospice the warm human contact he had never known - including a long-estranged sister who arrived from Canada following a phone call by Hospice staff, and sat with him every day until the end.

The way the authors present the lives and deaths of their fourteen participants makes the experience very real. There is a strong sense of their engagement with their subjects' lives, particularly, perhaps, on the part of Michael Young, who makes clear in the preface his own very personal involvement with cancer. This is no routine piece of social scientific research. It does not aim primarily to make a conceptual contribution to our understanding of dying, though it uses to very good effect ideas (those, for instance, of Murray Parkes, 1972, Kubler-Ross, 1989 and Marris, 1986) that are already familiar. Rather, it *shows* us what dying feels like. It is a humane and thoughtful book, rich in insights, by someone who has himself lived with death on very intimate terms.

REFERENCES

Kubler-Ross, E., *On Death and Dying*, Tavistock/Routledge, London 1989.

Marris, P., *Loss and Change*, (revised edition), Routledge, London 1986.

Murray Parkes, C., *Bereavement: studies of grief in adult life*, Penguin, Harmondsworth 1972.

Young, M. and Willmott, P., *Family and Kinship in East London*, Routledge and Kegan Paul, London 1957.

Soundings

SPECIAL ISSUE: AFTER THE ELECTION
Setting the Agenda in post-conservative Britain
September 1997 - 128pp FREE to subscribers

Soundings is a journal of politics and culture. It is a forum for ideas which aims to explore the problems of the present and the possibilities for a future politics and society. Its intent is to encourage innovation and dialogue in progressive thought. Half of each future issue will be devoted to debating a particular theme: topics in the pipeline include: 'Young Britain', Active Welfare in Britain, America, Africa, and The European Left.

Why not subscribe?
Make sure of your copy

Subscription rates, 1997 (3 issues)

INDIVIDUAL SUBSCRIPTIONS: UK - £35.00   *Rest of the World - £45.0*
INSTITUTIONAL SUBSCRIPTIONS UK - £70.00   *Rest of the World - £80.00*

Please send me one year's subscription starting with Issue Number _____

I enclose payment of £ _____

I wish to become a supporting subscriber and enclose a donation of £ _____

I enclose total payment of £ _____

Name _____

Address _____

_____

_____ Postcode _____

Please return this form with cheque or money order payable to Soundings and send to:

Soundings, c/o Lawrence & Wishart, 99A Wallis Road, London E9 5LN

A SPRING OFFER TO RISING EAST READERS
Travel & urban geography titles from Lawrence & Wishart

Each title is individually reduced or get ALL THREE for just £25.00 POSTFREE

Rising in the East: The Regeneration of East London
Tim Butler and Michael Rustin (eds)

Every modern global city needs its urban hinterland, and London has its ever expanding East End. This area now attracts huge volumes of public and private investment, in what has become the largest urban development zone in the United Kingdom. The East End now takes in a large part of Essex, on some definitions stretching as far as Southend; its population is one of the most ethnically diverse in Britain; it is becoming significantly more middle class; and its industrial base is shifting. This fascinating book of essays explores the meanings of these changes.

'An excellent series of essays' *Labour Euro News*
'Challenging and insightful' *IMA Agenda*

Special offer price £12.00 POSTFREE
Normal price £14.99pb (224pp)

Staying Close to the River: Reflections on Travel and Politics
Ken Worpole

Ken Worpole weaves a rich literary tapestry as he reflects on memories of friends and places he has known and loved. Through a unique series of letters, *Staying Close to the River* charts a route through four generations of family life, the political progress of the left, the cities of the world, and human fallibility. Both moving and funny, Ken's style is a testimony to the art of detailed evocation and meticulous observation, whether at home in the East End, sweating on the road to Tuscany, or discussing the arrival of 'Dallas' on Russian TV. This book is a rare gem.

'It's strange to discover something fresh in an age stale with literary invention, but Worpole pioneers a type of freewheeling epistolary travelogue'
Elizabeth Wilson, *The Guardian*

'It is a rough, idiosyncratic, touching diary.' *New Statesman*

Special offer price £8.00 POSTFREE
Normal price £9.99pb (192pp)

The Green London Way
Bob Gilbert

The first urban long-distance walk - a 92 mile route through the green spaces and commons of London, combining insights into the history of London's people with an in-depth knowledge of its land and wildlife.

'The Green London Way is admirably written, with stirring tales of how the citizenry banded together to save their priceless open spaces from the clutches of heartless developers.' Michael Leapman, *New Statesman*

'Bob Gilbert's philosophy is that city wildlife is just as exciting as the countryside, the book has a large fan following.' Nicola Baird, *BBC Wildlife*

'a refreshingly outspoken, well researched and opinionated critique.' *Time Out*

Special offer price £8.00 POSTFREE
Normal price £9.99pb (216pp)

YOU CAN PHOTOCOPY THIS FORM OR WRITE ON A SEPARATE SHEET - <u>ALL</u> DETAILS MUST BE INCLUDED
Please accompany your order with payment in Sterling either by cheque or Mastercard/Visa POSTFREE in the UK; £1 per book overseas.

Please send me [ ] copies of title [ ] offer price [ ]
I enclose a cheque for £ [ ] (made payable to Lawrence & Wishart)
OR Please debit my Mastercard/ Visa Card No [ ] Expiry Date [ ]
Name & Address* [ ]
[ ] Postcode [ ]
Telephone [ ] E-mail [ ]
* If paying by Mastercard/ Visa please give name and address as they appear on your statements

Return to: Lawrence & Wishart, 99a Wallis Road, London E9 5LN.
Tel: 0181 533 2506 Fax: 0181 533 7369. E-mail: orders@l-w-bks.demon.co.uk

[ ] **Lawrence & Wishart is an independent radical publisher, with titles ranging over cultural studies, politics, Education and gender. Please tick here if you would like to receive the 1997 Lawrence & Wishart Catalogue.**

RISING EAST

The aim of Rising East is to engage with the future development of East London, to give voice to its unique community and culture. It will explore the region's status as the biggest zone of regeneration in Europe and address the problems and challenges which affect the ethnically diverse population which lives and works amidst the new infrastructures.

Each issue will cover a variety of connected issues, looking at social and economic trends in the area, at policy research on regional strategy and at the rich cultural and artistic life of East London.

Rising East will be published three times a year. Future topics include: analysis of particular places and organisations - the LDDC and the Royal Docks, the Lee Valley, the new international station at Stratford; analyses of regional trends - in health, education and household structure; comparative perspectives on urban regeneration - in Barcelona and US cities; and reviews and articles on cultural life.

Why not subscribe?
Make sure of your copy

Subscription rates, 1997 (3 issues)

INDIVIDUAL SUBSCRIPTIONS		
UK	£20.00	Rest of the World £30.00
INSTITUTIONAL SUBSCRIPTIONS		
UK	£50.00	Rest of the World £60.00
CORPORATE SUBSCRIPTIONS		
UK	£100.00	Rest of the World £110.00

Please send me one year's subscription starting with Issue Number _____

I enclose payment of £ _____

Name _____

Address _____

_____

_____ Postcode _____

Please return this form with cheque or money order payable to *Rising East* and send to:
Rising East, c/o Lawrence & Wishart, 99A Wallis Road, London E9 5LN

European Initiative
Flying the Flag for London East

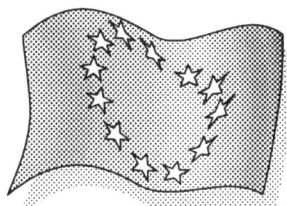

A Rising in the East is occurring with a sizeable contribution from the European Union. The late 1990s will see unprecedented levels of EU funding for regional economic development in London East. The *European Initiative*, a dedicated team of policy and programme advisers based at London East Training and Enterprise Council, offers organisations:

INFORMATION AND ADVICE

- Seminars on how to access development grants from Europe

  Assistance with applications and bid writing for projects which meet the needs of the London East region

- Briefings and information tools, including *LE Journal*, the quarterly European newsletter of London East

PARTNERSHIP DEVELOPMENT

- Administration of the *East London European Forum*, chaired by Carole Tongue, Member of the European Parliament for London East and Drew Stevenson, Professor of Urban Regeneration at the University of East London
- Leadership of the Thames Gateway London Partnership's European Group adding an EU dimension to the largest economic development opportunity in Western Europe
- Establishing working relations with partners from other EU Member States

PROJECT MANAGEMENT

- Management of EU-funded projects which underpin the strategic development objectives of London East and the Thames Gateway
- Implementation of systems to control, monitor and evaluate the use of European funding in local and regional projects

For further information on how you can access the products and services of the LETEC/LDDC *European Initiative*, contact Brenda Hunt on 0171 505 2471 or Kingsley Otubushin on 0171 505 2518

CARTWRIGHT CUNNINGHAM HASELGROVE and Co.

Solicitors

As North East London's leading law firm, CCH & Co. offers a high-quality yet cost-effective service to handle all legal affairs, both business and personal.

- Company and business matters
- Commercial and domestic conveyancing
- Matrimonial and family law
- Personal injury and medical negligence
- Contract disputes and debt collection
- Wills, probate and trusts
- Legal Aid
- Most other legal work

Phone us or call in for immediate help and a FREE initial discussion. Cost estimates provided.

LEYTON 618 Lea Bridge Road Road Leyton E10 6AT
Telephone 0181 539 4244   0181 556 8496
WALTHAMSTOW 282/284 Hoe Street Walthamstow E17 9QD
Telephone 0181 520 1021   0181 521 8838
WOODFORD 13 The Broadway Woodford Green Essex IG18 0HL
Telephone 0181 504 8802   0181 505 4227
CHINGFORD 233A Chingford Mount Road Chingford E4 8LP
Telephone 0181 524 2878   0181 529 8368

REGULATED BY THE LAW SOCIETY IN THE CONDUCT OF INVESTMENT BUSINESS